"Randy Alcorn's concise but comprehensive presentation of the pro-life position is an invaluable resource for openhearted—yet often tongue-tied—pro-lifers everywhere."

—Frederica Mathewes-Green
Columnist, commentator, and author of *Real Choices:*
Listening to Women, Looking for Alternatives to Abortion

"This compelling volume shatters stereotypes, and it will help heal the wounds of America's most urgent internal conflict."

—Rabbi Daniel Lapin
President of *Toward Tradition,* a national coalition of
Jews and Christians; author and radio talk show host

"A compelling case for the most important issue of our generation. I couldn't put it down."

—Andy Stanley
North Point Community Church

"To change our culture, it is not enough to say that we are pro-life; we must explain why we are pro-life. This book is an excellent resource that does precisely that."

—Fr. Frank Pavone
National Director, Priests for Life
President, National Pro-life Religious Council

"*Why Pro-Life?* is an invaluable resource for anyone trying to help a friend or family member understand the pro-life perspective. With clear, compelling language, Randy Alcorn lays out the case for life, using the power of both reason and emotion."

—Charles W. Colson
Founder, Prison Fellowship

P9-DCD-969

"A well-thought-out and thorough analysis of why protecting all human life is not only the right position but the only position we as a society should support. I believe minds will be changed after reading this book."

—Kristen Day

"All the proof anyone could need. Condensed into this tiny book are compelling answers to the most common pro-choice arguments. Randy Alcorn offers a powerful reminder that all created beings are deserving of dignity, freedom, and equal rights. I believe this book has the capacity to open the eyes and change the hearts of millions. A powerful book that you will want to give to everyone you know."

—Nancy Stafford
Actress and author of *The Wonder of His Love*
and *Beauty by the Book*
Executive Director, Democrats for Life of America

"A comprehensive, well-documented, and compelling book, particularly as it relates to our babies at risk."

—Jennifer O'Neill
Actress, author, and spokesperson for
Silent No More Awareness Campaign

Why Pro-Life?

caring for the unborn and their mothers

OTHER BOOKS BY RANDY ALCORN

FICTION

The Chasm
Edge of Eternity
Courageous
The Ishbane Conspiracy
Deadline
Lord Foulgrin's Letters
Dominion
Safely Home
Deception

NONFICTION

50 Days of Heaven
90 Days of God's Goodness
Does the Birth Control Pill Cause Abortions?
Eternal Perspectives: A Collection of Quotations on Heaven, the New Earth,
    and Life after Death
The Goodness of God
The Grace and Truth Paradox
Heaven
If God Is Good . . . Faith in the Midst of Suffering and Evil
In Light of Eternity
Law of Rewards
Life Promises for Eternity
Managing God's Money
Money, Possessions & Eternity
ProLife Answers to ProChoice Arguments
The Promise of Heaven
The Purity Principle
The Resolution for Men (with Alex and Stephen Kendrick)
Sexual Temptation: Establishing Guardrails and Winning the Battle
TouchPoints: Heaven
The Treasure Principle
We Shall See God

CHILDREN'S BOOKS

Heaven for Kids
Tell Me about Heaven
Wait until Then

Why Pro-Life?

caring for the unborn and their mothers

Revised and Updated

RANDY ALCORN

HENDRICKSON PUBLISHERS

Why Pro-Life? Caring for the Unborn and Their Mothers

© 2012 Hendrickson Publishers Marketing, LLC
P. O. Box 3473
Peabody, Massachusetts 01961-3473

ISBN 978-1-61970-028-4

Printed in the United States of America

Fourth Printing Revised and Updated Edition — May 2015

Library of Congress Cataloging-in-Publication Data

Alcorn, Randy C.
    Why pro-life? : caring for the unborn and their mothers / Randy Alcorn. — [Rev. ed.].
        p. cm.
    Rev. ed. of: Why prolife?
    Includes bibliographical references (p.   ).
    ISBN 978-1-61970-028-4 (alk. paper)
    1. Abortion—Moral and ethical aspects. 2. Abortion—Religious aspects—Christianity. 3. Right to life. I. Alcorn, Randy C. Why prolife? II. Title.
    HQ766.15.A53 2013
    205'.6976—dc23

                                2012031911

To Audrey Stout,
who cares for the unborn and their mothers,
and who cared for my mother when she was
dying of cancer in 1981.
Your acts of kindness will not be forgotten
by the God who rewards every cup of
cold water given in His name.

THANKS ...

... to my editor and valued friend, Rod Morris, for his fine touch-up work on the original book. To Cathy Ramey, who did a great job reducing my original manuscript and helping us update this 2012 revision; Stephanie Anderson, Kathy Norquist, and Julia Stager who helped with the 2012 revision; and Bonnie Hiestand, who typed in some of the final changes I made on hard copy.

Thanks to Brian Smith, Brent Rooney, Kristina Coulter, Kimberly Brock, and Brian Thomasson for their assistance on the original project; and to Doug Gabbert for his encouragement. Thanks to my wife, Nanci, Ron Norquist, Janet Albers, Linda Jeffries, and Sharon Misenhimer. I deeply appreciate each of you for your valuable partnership.

Many thanks also to Gayle Atteberry, Larry Gadbaugh, and Alice Gray, who gave me helpful input on the first draft.

Finally, my heartfelt thanks to Rick Brown and the fine people at Hendrickson Publishers for publishing my 2012 revision, expansion, and update.

CONTENTS

SECTION 4: OTHER IMPORTANT ISSUES

SECTION 5: SPIRITUAL PERSPECTIVES AND OPPORTUNITIES

APPENDICES

Author's Introduction to the Revised Edition

Why Pro-Life? was first published in 2004. With three hundred thousand English copies in print, and translations in eighteen other languages, I have been amazed at its far-reaching impact. We have heard many heart-warming stories about lives touched by the book.

But technology changes, statistics become dated, and new resources, stories, and discussions arise. It was time for a thorough update and revision.

As I write this in 2012, with the help of others—in particular, research assistant Cathy Ramey—I have gone over every sentence in the book, revising and updating. Hardly a paragraph of the original has remained unedited, and much new material has been added.

I am pleased to say that although I believe the original was a good book, the expanded and updated version is a better one. Those who read the original will find much more to think about and to use.

May this new book serve to further in greater ways the purposes for which it was originally written.

Randy Alcorn

Section I

THE
BASICS

Chapter 1

Why Talk
about Abortion?

Years ago a representative of what was then called the National Abortion Rights Action League spoke in a nearby public high school class on the merits of abortion. A student asked the teacher if I could come to present the pro-life position. When I arrived a week later, the pro-choice instructor informed me that his students had voted twenty-three to one for the pro-choice position.

I presented the case for the humanity and rights of unborn children. I showed intrauterine photographs demonstrating the development of the unborn at the earliest stages when abortions are performed. (This is far easier today when ultrasounds so graphically demonstrate what for decades—when there was no window to the womb—pro-choice advocates denied.)

After class, the teacher said to me, "If we were to vote again, the outcome would be different. Minds were changed." Then he added something remarkable, with some sadness in his eyes: "You know, until today I'd never heard the pro-life position."

Our schools pride themselves on being open-minded and providing a fair and fact-oriented education. Yet here was a fifty-five-year-old social science teacher with a master's degree who'd *never heard the pro-life position*. He had adopted the pro-choice position without scrutiny, and his students had done the same—until they saw and heard the truth.

The Surprising Trend

Not long ago, young people seemed so immersed in moral relativism and tolerance-driven postmodern culture, it appeared they

2

would eventually become uniformly pro-choice. But something happened. Now, surprisingly, more young people than their parents oppose abortion.

A 2003 Gallup survey of teenagers found that 72 percent believed abortion was morally wrong. Only 19 percent believed abortion should be legal in all circumstances, compared to 26 percent of adults. About 32 percent of teens, compared to 17 percent of adults, thought abortion should never be permitted.[1]

This was confirmed by a subsequent national poll, and evidenced by larger numbers of teenagers participating in the national March for Life. By 2010, Gallup updated their survey with the headline "The New Normal on Abortion: Americans More 'Pro-Life,' "[2] and in 2011 their polling revealed that by a 24 percent margin (61 to 37) Americans want most or all of abortions to be illegal.[3]

Youth webzines such as *The Advocate*[4] and youth-activist organizations have reported a sharp rise in teen/young adult opposition to abortion.[5] They have also been very instrumental in informing the general public about the dangers associated with abortion.[6] Contemporary websites reach out to young women, encouraging them to choose life.[7] Many young people are refusing to accept their culture's defense of abortion.

In *Why Pro-Life?* I'll present factual and compassionate reasons that explain and validate this movement away from the so-called pro-choice stance to a pro-life perspective.

The Defining Issue of Our Age

Abortion is America's most frequently performed surgery on women. The Guttmacher Institute, a polling agency for the abortion industry, reports that four out of every ten pregnancies are ended by abortion.[8] There are about 1.21 million reported abortions in the United States every year, down about 8 percent since 2000.[9]

Virtually every family, at some level, has been touched by abortion.

The stakes in this issue are extraordinarily high. If the pro-choice position is correct, the freedom to choose abortion is a basic civil right. If the pro-life position is correct, human casualties from

the 3,315 surgical abortions occurring in America (not even count-
ing chemical abortions, some of them from contraceptives) *every
day* total more than all lives lost in the September 11, 2001, destruction of the World Trade Center.

A recent Gallup poll indicated 27 percent of Americans say
they are very strongly pro-choice, while 22 percent say they are very
strongly pro-life. Taken together, that means 49 percent of Americans hold a strong view on abortion, either for or against.[10] The other
51 percent are not as firm in their opinions. However, even these
"uncertain" mostly believe that "abortion is morally wrong" and
39 percent of them favor restrictions in all but a select few circumstances. Hence, the majority of Americans still value life and can still
be influenced in their thinking about abortion.

A Christian Perspective

Some Christian readers may think, "This book isn't for us—we
don't have abortions, un-churched people do." In fact, 43 percent
of women obtaining abortions identify themselves as Protestant,
and 27 percent identify themselves as Catholic. So two-thirds of
America's abortions are obtained by those with a Christian affili-
ation. One of every five US abortions—about a quarter-million a
year—are performed on women who identify themselves as born-
again or evangelical Christians.[11]

Many church-attending women, younger and older, have had
abortions. Many church-attending men got those women pregnant
and either pressured, encouraged, or at least agreed with the mother
to abort their children.

The abortion issue isn't about the church needing to speak to
the world. It's about the church needing to speak to itself first, and
then to the world.

Though I'm a Christian, I don't make many arguments from
the Bible in the main body of this book. (I've done that elsewhere,[12]
and also deal with Scripture in this book's appendices.) The case I
present is grounded in medical science and reliable psychological
studies. These sources should be as credible to any truth-respecting
agnostic or atheist as they are to Christians.

I'm a strong believer in women's rights. I have the deepest respect for my wife and my daughters, whom we raised to respect themselves and to be grateful God made them female. I don't want to understate the trauma women have gone through in making abortion-related decisions. No one understands suffering like Jesus Christ, who is full of grace and truth. Chapter 19 on finding God's forgiveness is one I need as much as anyone.

This book presents facts and logic, infused with grace and compassion, that can help us root our beliefs in reality.

My Request of Readers

If you are pro-choice and reading a book titled *Why Pro-Life?* then good for you. I hope this means you have an open mind. If the pro-life side proves to be as senseless and irrational as you may have been led to believe, fine, you can give it the firsthand rejection it deserves. But if it proves to be sensible, then I encourage you to rethink your position.

If you're one of the 50 percent who are on the fence, with mixed feelings, I ask you to make this book part of your quest for truth. You can hear the pro-choice position anywhere—just turn on a TV or read the newspaper. But unless you read or listen to other viewpoints more widely than most people, this book may be your only opportunity to examine the pro-life position.

If you are pro-life, I also ask you to think through your position. It isn't good enough to say, "I know I'm right, but I'm not sure why." We should base our beliefs on the evidence. If we're wrong on any point, by all means let's revise our position. If we're right, we need to learn how to intelligently and graciously inform others.

One thing is certain: If abortion really does kill children and harm women, then there's too much at stake to remain silent and do nothing.

Chapter 2

Pro-Woman or Pro-Child?

My wife and I became involved in pro-life work out of concern for women who'd been devastated by abortion. In 1981 we opened our home to a pregnant teenage girl. I served on the board of one of the first pregnancy centers on the West Coast, with the objective of offering help and abortion-alternatives to pregnant women who were needy, confused, and desperate.

As time went on, I became involved in pro-life education, political action, and peaceful nonviolent intervention outside abortion clinics. Some pro-life ministries focus more on saving unborn children, others more on helping pregnant women. I found both kinds of efforts to be vitally necessary and completely compatible.

The Movement You May Not Know

Countless myths have been attached to the pro-life movement. One example is the oft-repeated statement, "Pro-lifers don't really care about pregnant women, or about children once they're born." A television reporter, with cameras rolling, approached me at a pro-life event and asked for my response to that accusation. I said, "Well, my wife and I opened our home to a pregnant girl and paid her expenses while she lived with us. We supported her when she decided to give up the child for adoption. And, since you asked, we give a substantial amount of our income to help poor women and children."

Then I introduced her to a pastor friend standing next to me who, with his wife, had adopted nineteen children, a number of them with Down syndrome and other special needs. The reporter signaled the cameraman to stop filming. I asked if she wanted to interview my friend. She shook her head and moved on, looking for someone who matched her stereotype of the pro-lifer who doesn't care about children once they're born.

The truth is, thousands of pro-life organizations around the country and throughout the world provide free pregnancy tests, ultrasounds, counseling, support groups, childcare classes, financial management education, babysitting, diapers, children's clothes, and housing. To these, add tens of thousands of churches donating time, money, food, house repairs, and every other kind of help to needy pregnant women, single mothers, and low-income families. Countless pro-lifers adopt children, open their homes, and volunteer to help children after they're born. Together, I am convinced these efforts actually comprise the single largest grassroots volunteer movement in history.

While those who offer abortions charge women for them, those who offer abortion alternatives give their assistance freely, lovingly, and almost entirely behind the scenes. Contrary to some caricatures, these people are not just pro-birth—they are truly pro-life. They care about a child and her mother, and help them both before birth and after.

Our National Schizophrenia

Despite the split among those calling themselves pro-choice and pro-life, well over two-thirds of Americans say they believe abortion is "morally wrong."[1] Some pro-life advocates believe this means it's no longer necessary to argue that the unborn is human or that abortion is wrong. Instead, our emphasis should be on helping women see that abortion isn't in their best interests. I emphatically agree we should help women.

Yet many women still believe that as bad as abortion may be, it is the lesser of evils, a better alternative than having a baby, raising a child, or surrendering a child for adoption.[2]

We must show the men and women indoctrinated to believe abortion is the best choice, that while the alternatives are challenging, only abortion kills an innocent person. Precisely because it does so, it has by far the most negative consequences in a woman's life.

Many of the same people who believe unborns are human and that abortion is immoral nonetheless choose to have abortions and defend abortion as legitimate. This proves they don't believe abortion is immoral in the same way that killing a three-month-old or a three-day-old is immoral.

Polls also indicate that many of the same people who believe abortion is immoral believe it should remain legal. This is odd. After all, surely they believe rape, kidnapping, child abuse, and murder are immoral—but they wouldn't argue that rape and murder should be legal. This demonstrates a fundamental difference between what they mean by rape and murder being "immoral" and abortion being "immoral."

No one who considers a preborn child a full-fledged person can rationally defend abortion's legality unless they also defend legalizing the killing of other human beings. After all, every argument for abortion that appeals to a mother's inconvenience, stress, and financial hardship can be made just as persuasively about her two-year-old, her teenager, her husband, or her parents. In many cases older children are *more* expensive and place *greater* demands on their mother than an unborn child. People immediately recognize those arguments as invalid when it comes to killing older children. So why not the unborn?

Women often say that when they got abortions they had no idea who was inside them. Some knew subconsciously they were carrying a child, but they latched on to dehumanizing pro-choice rhetoric that doesn't call an unborn baby a baby, but a "product of conception," an embryo, fetus, and sometimes even that old unscientific propaganda "blob of tissue."

Having discovered their mistake after their abortions, these women now profoundly regret being misled by abortion clinics who reassured them of what was untrue. They think of what they did as temporary insanity, usually enabled by their well-intentioned but misguided friends or family. They wish someone would have tried to talk them out of the choice that now haunts them. One woman, sobbing with guilt and regret, said to me, "I prayed that if I shouldn't get an abortion just one person would be standing outside the clinic when I came, to try to talk me out of it. But no one was there."

We should love and care for pregnant women who feel pressured toward abortion. We should also love women who've had abortions, and do all we can to help them recover from abortion's trauma.

The False Dichotomy

It's never in anyone's best interests to kill a child. It's not just the child who suffers, it's her mother.

Precisely because the unborn is a child, the consequences of killing him are severe. It's the identity of the first victim, the child, that brings harm to the second victim, the mother. That's why we need to begin our treatment of abortion by focusing on the true identity of the unborn.

Section 2

THE
CHILD

Chapter 3

Are the Unborn Really Human Beings?

P ro-choice advocates once commonly stated, "It's uncertain when human life begins; that's a religious question that cannot be answered by science." Most have abandoned this position because it's contradicted by decades of scientific evidence. However, this out-of-date belief is so deeply engrained in our national psyche that it's still widely believed.

Throughout history the words *fertilization* and *conception* have often been used interchangeably. Both referred to that time when egg and sperm joined into a single unified cell. Fertilization was the *process* by which the sperm penetrated the ovum. Conception was the *outcome* in which twenty-three chromosomes from a sperm cell joined with twenty-three chromosomes from an ovum to form a single unique life with its own distinctive DNA.

Political battles have long been fought over these two words, precisely because winning propaganda wars depends on semantic manipulation. Back in 1963 and 1965 pro-choice advocates within the US Department of Health, Education and Welfare (HEW) and the American College of Obstetricians and Gynecologists (ACOG) sought to normalize, or strip away the great historic resistance to, the notion of medically killing unborn children.

Redefining Conception

The promotion of "therapeutic abortion" (note the semantics of labeling killing as *therapeutic*) involved redefining the word *conception*. Rather than refer to the most immediate outcome of the fertilization process (usually within the first twenty-four hours of sperm-to-egg penetration), they determined to begin using "conception" to refer to a point at which the unborn child is approximately seven to eight days old.

What was once a process called "nidation" or "implantation" was, without public discourse, henceforth systematically referred to as "conception."

By using a word associated with the very beginning of life but referring to a point several days later in time, ACOG confused and desensitized not only the public, but even its medical colleagues.

Planned Parenthood's website assures questioners that emergency contraception doesn't cause abortions.

> Is it true that emergency contraception causes abortion? What about other hormonal methods of birth control?

> No. Abortion ends a pregnancy. Emergency contraception (EC) cannot end a pregnancy. EC works before a pregnancy begins. Pregnancy begins with the implantation of the developing fertilized egg in a woman's uterus.[1]

The truth is, though emergency contraceptives do not *always* cause abortions, sometimes they do. But by claiming that pregnancy begins with implantation, they convince people that an already conceived child's death is not an abortion.

Such definitions have caused even some pro-life advocates to confuse the distinctive processes of conception and implantation. Therefore, throughout this book I will use "fertilization" and "conception" in a historically accurate manner, referring to the earliest process and outcome of human life's beginning.

What Science Says

Dr. Alfred M. Bongiovanni, then professor of obstetrics at the University of Pennsylvania, stated, "I have learned from my earliest medical education that human life begins at the time of conception . . . human life is present throughout this entire sequence from conception to adulthood . . . any interruption at any point throughout this time constitutes a termination of human life."

Speaking of the early stages of a child's development in the womb, as far back as 1981, in testimony before a congressional sub-committee, Professor Bongiovanni said, "I am no more prepared to say that these early stages represent an incomplete human being than I would be to say that the child prior to the dramatic effects of puberty is not a human being. This is human life at every stage."[2]

Dr. Jerome LeJeune, while genetics professor at the University of Descartes in Paris, stated, "After fertilization has taken place a new human being has come into being." He said, this "is no longer a matter of taste or opinion. Each individual has a very neat beginning, at conception."[3]

Harvard University Medical School Professor Micheline Matthews-Roth said, "It is scientifically correct to say that an individual human life begins at conception."

The moment of each person's creation is the moment of conception. Before that moment the individual (with her unique DNA) does not exist, after that moment she does.

No Question, It's A Fact

It's not only pro-life people who believe this. The owner of Oregon's largest abortion clinic testified under oath, *"Of course* human life begins at conception." The award-winning secular book *From Conception to Birth* documents the child's beginning at conception and her movement toward birth, as do other books and DVDs.[4]

How clear is the proof that human life begins at conception? There are a multitude of historic authorities,[5] so many that the Missouri General Assembly overwhelmingly approved a 2003 bill that stated, "The general assembly of this state finds that: (1) The life of each human being begins at conception; (2) Unborn children have protectable interests in life, health, and well-being. . . . The term 'unborn children' or 'unborn child' shall include all unborn child or children or the offspring of human beings from the moment of conception until birth at every stage of biological development."[6]

That life begins when the ovum and sperm unite into a single cell (called a *zygote*; from Greek, meaning "to join" or "to yoke") is a fact constantly in need of reaffirmation. Why? Because in

Roe v. Wade the US Supreme Court chose to ignore or act in defiance of overwhelming scientific evidence. They handed down a decision favoring a US Population Commission goal to reduce fertility and birth rates in the United States. In the divide between science and policy, the government sought out Planned Parenthood for guidelines, then began to implement that agency's suggested population control policy as represented in what is referred to as "the Jaffe memo."[7]

In spite of the historic deception that was embodied in *Roe v. Wade*, science continues to affirm what it has all along—that life begins at fertilization, or conception, which refer to the same starting point.[8]

What The Constitution Says

The Fourteenth Amendment says that the state shall not deprive any person of life without due process of law. When that was written, the word *human* was a synonym for *person* and could just as easily have been used. The Supreme Court admitted in *Roe v. Wade*: "If the suggestion of personhood [of the unborn] is established, the appellant's [pro-abortion] case, of course, collapses, for the fetus's right to life is then guaranteed specifically by the [fourteenth] amendment."[9]

To solve this problem, the court chose to abandon the historic meaning of personhood. In the years that have followed, a long series of subjective and artificial distinctions have been made by pro-choice advocates to differentiate between *humans* and *persons*. Part of the reason for this is that the scientific fact that life begins at conception paints the pro-choice movement into a corner. The newer strategy is to say, "Okay, this is human life, but it isn't really a person."

Changing the meaning of words doesn't change reality. The concept of personhood is now virtually worthless as an ethical guide in the matter of abortion. The only objective questions we can ask are

"Is it human; that is, did it come from human beings?"

"Is it a genetically unique individual?"

"Is it alive and growing?"

If the answers are yes, then "it" is in fact a "he" or "she," a living person, possessing rights and deserving of legal protection.

What A Pro-Abortion Ethicist Says

Consider carefully these words written by a father concerning his son:

> On the desk in my office . . . there are several pictures of my son, Eli. In one, he is gleefully dancing on the sand along the Gulf of Mexico, the cool ocean breeze wreaking havoc with his wispy hair. In the second, he is tentatively seated in the grass in his grandparents' backyard, still working to master the feat of sitting up on his own. In a third, he is only a few weeks old, clinging firmly to the arms that are holding him and still wearing the tiny hat for preserving body heat that he wore home from the hospital. Through all these remarkable changes that these pictures preserve, he remains unmistakably the same little boy.
>
> In the top drawer of my desk, I keep another picture of Eli. This picture was taken on September 7, 1993, 24 weeks before he was born. The sonogram image is murky, but it reveals clearly enough a small head tilted backward slightly, and an arm raised up and bent, with the hand pointing back toward the face and the thumb extended out toward the mouth. There is no doubt in my mind that this picture, too, shows the same little boy at a very early stage in his physical development. And there is no question that the position I defend in this book entails that it would have been morally permissible to end his life at this point.[10]

Complex and Human

The newly fertilized egg contains a staggering amount of genetic information, sufficient to control the individual's growth and development for his entire lifetime. A single thread of DNA from a human cell contains information equivalent to a library of one thousand volumes.[11] Today we know the human genome has up to three billion base pairs of DNA that influence the expression of traits in an individual cell.[12]

The cells of the new individual divide and multiply rapidly, resulting in phenomenal growth. There's growth because there's life. Long before a woman knows she's pregnant, there is within her a living, growing human being.

Between five and nine days after conception the new person burrows into the womb's wall for safety and nourishment. Already his or her gender can be determined by scientific means. By fourteen days the child produces a hormone that suppresses the mother's menstrual period. It will be two more weeks before clearly human features are discernible and three more before they're obvious. Still, she is a full-fledged member of the human race.

At conception the unborn doesn't appear human to us who are used to judging humanity by everyday appearances. Nevertheless, in the objective scientific sense she is every bit as human as any older child or adult. In fact, *she looks just like a human being ought to look at her stage of development.*

At eighteen days after conception the heart is forming and eyes start to develop. By twenty-one days the heart pumps blood throughout the body. By twenty-eight days the unborn has budding arms and legs. By thirty days she has a brain and has multiplied in size ten thousand times.

By thirty-five days her mouth, ears, and nose are taking shape. At forty days the preborn child's brain waves can be recorded, and her heartbeat, which began three weeks earlier, can be detected by an ultrasonic stethoscope. By forty-two days her skeleton is formed and her brain is controlling the movement of muscles and organs.

No matter how he or she looks, a child is a child. Abortion terminates that child's life. The earliest means to cause abortion, including Mifepristone (RU-486) and all abortion pills, take a human life just as certainly as if the life taken were that of a week-old, year-old, or twenty-year-old person.

The Drama of Life

Famous intrauterine photographer pioneer Lennart Nilsson is best known for his classic photo essays in *Life* magazine and his book, *A Child Is Born.* In his "Drama of Life before Birth," he says this of the unborn at forty-five days after conception (before many women know they're pregnant): "Though the embryo now weighs only 1/30 of an ounce, it has all the internal organs of the adult in various stages of development. It already has a little mouth with lips, an early tongue and buds for 20 milk teeth. Its sex and reproductive organs have begun to sprout."[13]

By eight weeks hands and feet are almost perfectly formed. By nine weeks a child will bend fingers around an object placed in the palm. Fingernails are forming, and the child is sucking his thumb. The nine-week baby has "already perfected a somersault, backflip and scissor kick."[14]

The unborn responds to stimulus and may already be capable of feeling pain.[15] Yet abortions on children at this stage are called "early abortions."

By ten weeks the child squints, swallows, and frowns. By eleven weeks he urinates, makes a wide variety of facial expressions, and even smiles.[16] By twelve weeks the child is kicking, turning his feet, curling and fanning his toes, making a fist, moving thumbs, bending wrists, and opening his mouth.[17]

All this happens in the first trimester, the first three months of life. In the remaining six months in the womb, nothing new develops or begins functioning. The fully intact child only grows and matures—unless her life is lost by spontaneous miscarriage or taken through abortion.

It's an indisputable scientific fact that *each and every surgical abortion stops a beating heart and stops already measurable brain waves.*

What do we call it when a person no longer has a heartbeat or brain waves? Death.

What should we call it when there *is* a heartbeat and there *are* brain waves? Life.

Every abortion ends a human life. That is a simple and scientifically certain fact.

SLED

Scott Klusendorf of Life Training Institute points out that there are only four differences between a preborn and a newborn. They can be remembered through the acronym SLED,[18] which I'll briefly summarize:

Size: Does how big you are determine who you are?

Level of development: Are twenty-year-olds more human than ten-year-olds, since they are smarter and stronger?

Environment: Does being inside a house make you more or less of a person than being outside? Does being located in his mother's body rather than outside make a child less human?

Degree of dependency: Does dependence upon another determine who you are? Is someone with Alzheimer's or on kidney dialysis less of a person? (Am I, an insulin-dependent diabetic, less of a person than before I developed the disease in 1985?)

A three-month-old is much smaller than a ten-year-old, far less developed, and just as incapable of taking care of himself as an unborn.

The question is not how old or big or smart or inconvenient the unborn are, but *who* they are.

The answer is simple: they are human beings.

Chapter 4

What's the Difference Between Egg, Sperm, Embryo, and Fetus?

Two years before abortion was legalized in America, a pro-choice advocate instructed nurses in a prominent medical journal, "Through public conditioning, use of language, concepts and laws, the idea of abortion can be separated from the idea of killing."[1]

The same year, a Los Angeles symposium added this to their training: "If you say, 'Suck out the baby,' you may easily generate or increase trauma; say instead, 'Empty the uterus,' or 'We will scrape the lining of the uterus,' but never, 'We will scrape away the baby.' "[2]

Language isn't just the *expression* of minds but the *shaper* of minds. How words are used influences our receptivity to an idea—even an idea that, communicated in straightforward terms, would be unthinkable.

Words that focus on the pregnancy and the uterus draw attention away from the person residing in the uterus. But no matter how we say it, "terminating a pregnancy" remains exactly what it is—taking a human life, killing a baby.

One pro-life feminist says, "Pro-lifers don't object to terminating pregnancies. Pregnancies are only supposed to last a short while. We favor terminating them at around nine months. The objection is to killing children."[3]

What Does Fetus Mean?

Like *toddler* and *adolescent,* the terms *embryo* and *fetus* don't refer to nonhumans but to humans at particular stages of development. *Fetus* is a Latin word variously translated "offspring," "young one," or "little child."

It's scientifically inaccurate to say a human embryo or a fetus is not a human being simply because he's at an earlier stage of development than an infant. This is like saying that a toddler isn't a human being because he's not yet an adolescent.

I have five grandchildren, born over a span of eight years. Are the older ones more human and the younger less human? Does someone become more human as they get bigger? If so, then adults are more human than children, and football players are more human than jockeys.

Something nonhuman doesn't become human by getting older and bigger; whatever is human must be human from the beginning.

Is Egg or Sperm a Person?

Carl Sagan once ridiculed abortion opponents by asking, "Why isn't it murder to destroy a sperm or an egg?"[4] As every scientist should know, there is a fundamental difference between sperm and unfertilized eggs on the one hand, and fertilized eggs or human zygotes on the other.

Like cells of one's hair or heart, neither egg nor sperm has the capacity to become other than what it is. But when egg and sperm are joined, a new, dynamic, and genetically unique human life begins. A fertilized egg is in fact *a newly conceived human being*. It is a *person*, with a life of his or her (not its) own, on a rapid pace of self-directed development.

From the instant of fertilization, that first single cell contains that child's entire genetic blueprint in all its complexity. This accounts for every detail of human development, including the child's gender, hair and eye color, height, and skin tone.[5] Take that single cell of the just conceived zygote, put it next to a chimpanzee cell, and "a geneticist could easily identify the human. Its humanity is already that strikingly apparent."[6]

The Power of Labels

"Product of conception," or POC, is a common depersonalization of the unborn child. In reality, the infant, the ten-year-old, and the adult are all "products of conception," no more nor less than the fetus. As the product of a horse's conception is always a horse, the product of human conception is always a human.

You and I are products of conception in *exactly* the same way a newly conceived child is. Of course we don't *call* each other POCs, because we recognize each other's humanity. Yet the unborn's humanity is no more dependent upon another's recognition of it than a slave's or Jew's humanity depended upon the plantation owners' or Nazis' recognition.

The debate about embryonic stem cells is an example of semantic power. Stem cells are versatile master cells from which a variety of tissues and organs develop. Considered prime materials for biomedical research, they're available from benign human sources, including consenting adults, umbilical cord blood, and placentas.[7] But many scientists are determined to use stem cells from embryonic human babies who lose their lives in the harvesting. This has serious implications for how we view human beings and whether or not they're expendable to serve others.[8]

Numerous medical and scientific organizations use fetal stem cells in their own research. These include The American Cancer Society, MacMillan Cancer Support, Juvenile Diabetes Foundation, and many others.[9]

Clouding the Semantic Waters

The National Institutes of Health (NIH) found that the public was reacting against "human embryonic stem cell research," destroying human embryos by experimentation. The solution? Reevaluating the ethics of what they were doing? No. The NIH simply chose a new term to describe exactly the same thing: "human pluripotent stem cell research." The new term was used to mask the reality that human embryos are the objects of experimentation.[10] Rather than discontinue an unethical procedure, they simply renamed it.

Avoiding controversy over the destruction of human life involves language, but it also involves creating distance in other ways. The NIH website stresses that embryonic stem cells used in their research "have been fertilized *in vitro*—in an *in vitro* fertilization clinic . . . not derived from eggs fertilized in a woman's body."[11] They focus on a lab *process* in order to deflect criticism.

No matter how a human embryo comes to be—through intercourse, rape, artificial insemination, or in a petri dish—a human embryo is still a human being in every sense of the term.

I know people conceived by artificial insemination and by rape. (Whether or not you realize it, it's likely you do too.) I guarantee you that neither they nor anyone who knows them has ever questioned their humanity.

Dr. Seuss puts it this way in the epilogue of his marvelous *Horton Hears a Who!* (a pro-life book if there ever was one): "So let that be a lesson to one and to all; a person's a person, no matter how small."[12]

No Doubts

If human cloning ever succeeds, a person would enter the life continuum at a point after conception.[13] This would do nothing to change their human status. It's a person's *presence* on the human life continuum, not how they arrived there, that matters.

Obstetrician Thomas Hilgers, who has devoted his career to helping women and saving lives, states, "No individual living body can 'become' a person unless it already is a person. No living being can become anything other than what it already essentially is."[14]

Having witnessed the changing tactics of pro-choice advocates over the decades, it's interesting to me that some abortion providers now admit what happens in an abortion, both early in pregnancy and later.

In 2011 and 2012 pro-choice activists decried attempts to promote "personhood" legislation for the unborn, which would make the Bill of Rights applicable to *all* human beings.

Their opposition is based on the fact that "some [contraceptive] methods may work, in part at least, by making the uterus inhospitable to implantation by a fertilized egg" according to Dr. Deborah Gilboa, a Pittsburgh family practice physician. "That could mean that some eggs become fertilized and are flushed out [aborted] in women taking a birth control pill, using an intrauterine device (IUD) or taking 'Plan B,' the morning-after pill."[15]

In other words, since they know human life begins at conception, some abortion advocates fear any legislation that extends human rights to all humans.

Dr. Warren Hern, long known for specializing in second- and third-trimester abortions, describes his work:

> I began an abortion on a young woman who was 17 weeks pregnant. . . . Then I inserted my forceps into the uterus and applied them to the head of the fetus, which was still alive, since fetal injection is not done at that stage of pregnancy. I closed the forceps, crushing the skull of the fetus, and withdrew the forceps. The fetus, now dead, slid out more or less intact.[16]

Those opposed to defining what "person" means in the Bill of Rights, as well as Dr. Hern, who has dedicated his life to performing abortions and teaching others how to do them, have absolutely no doubt that abortion kills a child.

Do you think you know something they don't?

Chapter 5

Is an Unborn Child Part
of the Mother's Body?

As have many others, philosopher Mortimer Adler claimed that the unborn is "a part of the mother's body, in the same sense that an individual's arm or leg is a part of the living organism. An individual's decision to have an arm or a leg amputated falls within the sphere of privacy."[1]

In 2003 Connecticut's high court ruled "that a fetus is part of the mother's body." At the same time that an American Medical Association newsletter reported the decision, it also noted that the Supreme Court handed down a concurrent ruling with one justice concluding, "A fetus may not have its own independent existence," then asserting "a fetus may be both 'a part of its mother as well as its own individual being.'"[2]

Well, which is it?

True or False?

A body part is defined by the common genetic code it shares with the rest of its body. Every cell of the mother's tonsils, appendix, heart, and lungs shares the same genetic code. The unborn child also has a genetic code, but it is distinctly different from his mother's. Every cell of his body is uniquely his, different from every cell of his mother's body. Often his blood type is also different and half the time his gender is different.

The new human being, in order to prevent being rejected as foreign by the mother's antibodies, must produce a special enzyme beginning on the sixth day or be destroyed.[3] The enzyme (indoleamine-2,3-dioxygenase), abbreviated IDO, suppresses the mother's T-cell production so that on day seven the embryonic child may attach to the mother's womb for nourishment.[4] If the embryo fails to produce IDO, it will die. Why? Because he is a distinct and different body inside the body of his mother.

People argue with a straight face that the woman's is the only body involved in a pregnancy. But if that is true, then consider the body parts this woman must have: two noses, four legs, two different sets of fingerprints, two brains—and half the time, she must also have male genitals. If it is impossible for a woman to have male genitals, then the boy she is carrying *cannot* be part of her body.

Separate and Equal

A Chinese zygote implanted in a Swedish woman will always be Chinese, not Swedish, because his identity is based on his genetic code, not that of the body in which he resides.

A child may die and the mother live, or the mother may die and the child live, proving they are two separate individuals.[5]

In prenatal surgeries, the unborn, still connected to the mother by the umbilical cord, is removed, given anesthesia, operated on, and reinserted into the mother's womb.[6] (The reason that the babies are given anesthesia in these surgeries has far reaching implications regarding abortions; it is precisely because the unborn child feels pain.) The child is called a patient, is operated on, and has her own medical records indicating blood type and vital signs.

In 1999 an unborn child named Samuel Armas was operated on for spina bifida. His photograph in *Life* magazine captured the world's attention. As the surgeon was closing the incision, Baby Samuel pushed his hand out of the womb and grabbed the surgeon's finger. Photojournalist Michael Clancy caught this astonishing act on film.[7] Clancy reported:

> Suddenly, an entire arm thrust out of the opening, then pulled back until just a little hand was showing. The doctor reached over and lifted the hand, which reacted and squeezed the doctor's finger. As if testing for strength, the doctor shook the tiny fist. Samuel held firm. I took the picture! Wow![8]

Samuel Armas was sewn back into his mother's womb and delivered nearly four months later. How did seeing Samuel grab the surgeon's finger affect Clancy? "In that instant Clancy went from being pro-choice to being pro-life. As he put it, 'I was totally in shock for two hours after the surgery. . . . I know abortion is wrong now—it's absolutely wrong.' "⁹

Does anyone seriously believe that this pain-feeling, finger-grabbing patient was simply an appendage of his mother's body? Can it be credibly argued that once he's placed back inside his mother, it should be legal to kill that same patient anytime during the remaining four months before he's born?

We All Know Better

At the Medical University of South Carolina, if a pregnant woman's urine test indicates cocaine use, she can be arrested for distributing drugs to a minor. Similarly, in Illinois a pregnant woman who takes an illegal drug can be prosecuted for "delivering a controlled substance to a minor." That taking these drugs while pregnant is a felony gives explicit recognition of the unborn as a person with rights, deserving protection even from his mother.

How ironic that the same woman who's prosecuted and jailed for endangering her child is perfectly *free to hire a doctor to abort that same child.* In America today it's illegal to harm your preborn child, but it's perfectly legal to kill her.

Every alcohol-serving establishment in Oregon is required to post this sign:

Pregnancy & Alcohol DO NOT MIX
Drinking alcoholic beverages, including wine coolers and beer, during pregnancy can cause birth defects.

I'll never forget the first time I saw this sign in a restaurant. My jaw dropped. For years I had publicly taken a stand very unpopular in Oregon—that the unborn are actually children and we should protect them. But this sign, clearly depicting a real baby inside his mother, warns women not to harm that baby.

But if the mother drinking alcohol harms her unborn child, what does abortion do to him?

Safe In Prison

In the year 2000 the US House of Representatives voted unanimously to delay capital punishment of a pregnant woman until after delivery.

By a vote of 417 to 0, the bill mandated that no state or federal authority, including the military, may "carry out a sentence of death on a woman while she carries a child *in utero*. . . . 'child *in utero*' means a member of the species homo sapiens, at any stage of development, who is carried in the womb."[10]

The most telling part of the vote was that not a single member of Congress opposed it. Every one, even the many who call themselves "pro-choice," *knew without a doubt* that unborn babies are *not* part of their mothers' bodies. They knew that *unborn children have rights independent of their mothers' rights*, and that they deserve the law's protection regardless of what their mothers have done.

No stay of execution was sought or legislated for the sake of the mother's tonsils, heart, or kidneys. The authorities intervened not for any part of the woman's body, but only for the innocent human being—with his own body—inside the woman.

So, are the three thousand plus unborn babies killed by abortion each day any less human or less deserving of protection than the child whom the US Congress intervened to save?

Do you see the irony? Under the law, the only absolutely protected unborn child in America is one whose mother is on death row!

Many states have passed fetal homicide laws, declaring it murder for anyone but the mother to deliberately take the life of a preborn child. These laws are explicit affirmations that the child is a human being. In 2004 Congress passed the "Unborn Victims of

Violence Act," which states that someone who "intentionally kills or attempts to kill the unborn child . . . [should] be punished . . . for intentionally killing or attempting to kill a human being."[11]

Consider the bizarre implications of this double standard. If a woman is scheduled to get an abortion but on her way to the abortion clinic her baby is killed *in utero*, the baby's killer will be prosecuted for murder. But if this murder does not occur, then one hour later a doctor can be paid to perform a legal procedure killing *exactly the same child* (in a way that is almost certainly more gruesome).

To the child, what's the difference who kills her? What consolation will she find in being killed legally rather than illegally?

A Lesson from Louise Brown

Being inside something isn't the same as being part of something. (A car isn't part of a garage because it's parked there.) Louise Brown, the first "test-tube baby," was conceived in 1978 when her father's sperm and mother's egg were joined in a petri dish. Did she become part of her mother's body when she was placed in her uterus? No. Neither had she been part of the petri dish when she lived there!

Human beings shouldn't be discriminated against because of their place of residence. The child's nature doesn't magically change in the twenty inches between the uterus and the birthing room.

Chapter 6

What Do the Pictures Tell Us?

The preborn child's biggest disadvantage used to be that there was no window to the womb. His fate was in the hands of those who could not see him. But in recent years this has radically changed.

In 2002 and 2003 *Time* magazine and *Newsweek* devoted cover stories to the breathtaking ultrasound images of preborn children.[1] *Newsweek* asked on its cover, "Should a Fetus Have Rights? How Science Is Changing the Debate." A decade later, *Newsweek* reports that the question remains a hotly debated issue.[2]

But for anyone willing to take a look, all arguments vaporize in the face of the unborn child.

The Power of Ultrasound

Rebekah Nancarrow received an eighty-dollar ultrasound at Planned Parenthood but wasn't allowed to see the results because, she was told, "that will only make it harder on you." At a Pregnancy Resource Center she was given a free ultrasound and allowed to view it. She said, "Had I not had the sonogram, I would have had the abortion. But that sonogram just confirmed 100 percent to me that this was a life within me, not a tissue or a glob."[3]

According to Thomas Glessner, lawyer and author of *The Emerging Brave New World*,[4] "Prior to ultrasound technology, pregnancy centers reported that of the 'abortion-minded' women who came in for testing and advice, about 20 percent to 30 percent decided to remain pregnant. With pregnancy centers using ultrasound machines, that proportion has jumped to 80 percent or 90 percent."[5] More recent surveys place the number of women who choose to remain pregnant after viewing an ultrasound of their baby at anywhere from 60 to 98 percent.[6]

Audrey Stout, a nurse, told me of one ultrasound she performed. This particular time the baby "opened and closed her mouth, had the hiccups, lay back as if in a beach chair, stretching her little legs. She even held up hands so Mom could count her fingers. The mother was visibly touched."

When Audrey finished the scan she asked the woman what her plans were. "She replied, 'I'm going to have my baby.'" Audrey asked if the scan had made a difference; she said, "'Big-time. I just came in here to get a pregnancy verification so I could go have an abortion.'"[7]

Thousands of stories like this have emerged from pregnancy centers that now use ultrasound. Internet sites display astounding images; some clearly show the unborn smiling, yawning, stretching, and sleeping.

No Tricks, Just Truth

I highly recommend that you take a few minutes now and view some 3D ultrasound images; www.prenatalpeek. com/3dultrasoundphotos/ is not a pro-life site; it's simply a business catering to customers who want prenatal photos of their unborn children. Yet these photographs have sufficient power that, were our culture thinking correctly, they would end the abortion debate in a heartbeat! (To see intrauterine videos of children at various levels of development, see www.ehd.org/.)

I will never forget showing an intrauterine photograph of an eight-week unborn child to a pro-choice advocate, an intelligent college graduate. She looked at me, disgust apparent, and asked, "Do you really think you're going to fool anyone with this *trick photography*?"

This was before the days of 3D ultrasounds, but I told her she could go to Harvard University Medical School textbooks, *Life* magazine,[8] or Nilsson's *A Child Is Born*[9] and find exactly the same pictures. She didn't want to hear it. The reason was obvious. She was really saying, "That's obviously a child, and because I don't want to believe abortion kills a child, I refuse to believe that's a real photograph."

This denial remains in spite of the explosion of 3D/4D technologies. When I posted some ultrasound images on my blog and

Facebook page, someone left a comment that they suspected these pictures had been "photoshopped." Why? *Because they looked like exactly what they really are—children!*

In March 2011, Kellie Copeland, representing NARAL (National Abortion Rights Action League) Pro-Choice America, testified before the Ohio legislature. Concerning pro-lifers who submitted ultrasound images, she stated, "I think it was a stunt." She regarded the showing of actual unedited film of unborn children in the womb as "a circus," a political trick aimed at swaying the hearings committee.[10]

Pro-choice advocates often mock pro-lifers. But who is rejecting reality to remain in denial? Do ultrasound images lie? Or do people tell lies to convince us that the scientific evidence isn't really saying what every objective person can see it is saying—that these are *babies* in the womb, and that therefore abortion kills babies.

What The Remains Indicate

A film called *The Gift of Choice* claims that the unborn is "a probability of a future person." But anyone who has dared to look knows what's left after an abortion: small but perfectly formed body parts—arms and legs, hands and feet, torso and head. The physical remains indicate the end not of a *potential* life but of an *actual* life. If you don't believe this, examine the remains of an abortion.[11]

Go online and view undercover interviews in which abortion clinic staff admit it is a "baby" that dies in an abortion.[12] If you cannot bear to look, ask yourself why. If this were only tissue rather than a dismembered child, it wouldn't be hard to look at, would it?

In his how-to manual, *Abortion Practice,* Dr. Warren Hern states, "A long curved Mayo scissors may be necessary to decapitate and dismember the fetus."[13] One must have a head in order to be decapitated and body parts in order to be dismembered. Lumps of flesh and blobs of tissue aren't decapitated or dismembered. Human beings are.

Why are the same people who watch bloody killings and gruesome autopsies in prime-time dramas disturbed by abortion photographs? Pro-choice feminist and author Naomi Wolf, speaking of pictures of aborted babies, acknowledges:

To many pro-choice advocates, the imagery is revolting propaganda. There is a sense among us, let us be frank, that the gruesomeness of the imagery belongs to the pro-lifers . . . that it represents the violence of imaginations that would, given half a chance, turn our world into a scary, repressive place. "People like us" see such material as the pornography of the pro-life movement. But feminism at its best is based on what is simply true. . . . While images of violent fetal death work magnificently for pro-lifers as political polemic, the pictures are not polemical in themselves: they are biological facts. We know this."[14]

See For Yourself

I hate doing it, but every so often I force myself to look at the photos again, to remind me of the terrible truth that *abortion kills children.*

Why not resolve this question in your own mind by viewing both the ultrasound photos and videos, and also the abortion visuals? For instance, see http://bit.ly/bHAcWR.

One online video shows live footage of an early abortion, at seven weeks. It is shocking. Sickening. Revolting. And precisely accurate. Because it shows a close-up of female genitals some might regard it as pornographic; I hesitate to link to it. However, so much is at stake, I believe every woman should consider seriously watching and seeing, unedited, exactly what happens in even an early abortion.[15]

I would ask every reader, male and female, to go to a website created by young people who oppose abortion: www.abort73.com/videos.

The two-minute and five-minute abortion overviews contain no trick photography, no embellishment, no propaganda, but actual photos of the remains of an abortion.

If you absolutely cannot bring yourself to look at the visual evidence, watch the five-minute version of the overview of abortion where the graphic parts are pixelated so they can't be seen.

If you really defend the pro-choice position and are an honest person, then you *must* be able to look at the photos and videos of abortions. Only then would you be defending something you have *seen* with your own eyes.

Censored Evidence

I was on a television program where pro-choice and pro-life advocates were discussing abortion. After we'd been talking a few minutes, one of the pro-lifers tried to illustrate his point by showing a picture of an aborted baby. As soon as he did, there were audible gasps, people started waving their arms, and the pro-choice activist next to me cried out, "God, don't let them show that!"

The cameras turned quickly away, and there was momentary panic and confusion in the studio. The person showing the actual photograph of a real aborted baby was admonished that this was not going to be permitted.

Had the issue not been so serious, the response would have been humorous. In what other debate would showing a photograph of the actual matter being discussed be considered out of bounds?

The picture of the baby was no more gruesome than pictures of Holocaust victims that appear in countless documentaries. And it was just as authentic. It simply showed what abortion is and what is left of the unborn baby when it's done.

I received a phone call from a college professor who was invited to participate in a debate in which he would defend the pro-life position and a colleague the pro-choice position. The only stipulation was this: "Neither side can show any pictures."

This sounded very fair to the professor who called me, who hadn't publicly addressed the issue before. "After all," he said, "both sides have to abide by the same rule."

My question was, "What pictures would someone taking the pro-choice position *want* to show?"

Imagine a debate about whether the Holocaust really happened. Supposedly in the interests of fairness, the Holocaust believer and the Holocaust denier are both given the same rule: "Neither of you can show pictures." The result? One side is deprived of its most persuasive proof, while the other side is spared from having to explain pictures demonstrating the fatal flaw in its argument.

As counterintuitive as it seems, anyone who has participated in abortion debates knows that it's typical to be told you cannot show pictures of aborted babies. (I've even been told that I couldn't show intrauterine photographs of the unborn.) Apparently people shouldn't be burdened with factual information that could influence their decision!

I have had to say, as winsomely as possible, "So you're pro-choice about abortion, but you're anti-choice about me presenting the evidence against abortion?"

Let The Truth Speak For Itself

Pro-life advocates invite their opponents to present their best evidence, and make their most persuasive case. We only ask that we be allowed to do the same. When one side in a debate insists on not allowing the other side to present critical evidence, what does it suggest about the weakness of their position? Why not lay all the evidence out on the table, and let people decide for themselves?

If the "fetus" is simply a blob of tissue, then fine—let the public see the blob of tissue. Let them be treated like adults and allowed to choose what they believe. From the pro-abortion perspective, if this is not a baby, *what could be the harm in looking at the pictures?*

Won't the truth serve only the position that is true?

The success of the pro-choice position is dependent on the public's refusal to believe that abortion kills children. The pictures are a devastating challenge to this denial, and they constitute a grave threat to the debate. Why? Because when the photos are examined objectively, the pro-choice argument collapses like a house of cards.

Can you imagine setting up a debate between whalers and animal rights activists, then informing the latter that they would not be permitted to show pictures of harpooned whales or clubbed seals?

Suppose I set up a debate about the effects of cigarette smoking, then stipulated that neither side would be allowed to present any visual evidence. Wouldn't you have reason to question my sincerity and honesty? (And perhaps reason to suspect that I am not interested in a real debate, but am working for the tobacco industry?)

It is a perplexing reality that this denial of the evidence, this refusal to show people what is actually true, has become an accepted part of the public debate (making it into a non-debate) about abortion. What is even more bewildering is that this approach, decades ago, spread to the practice of medicine. Consider this advice in a national publication for obstetricians and gynecologists:

> Sonography in connection with induced abortion may have psychological hazards. Seeing a blown-up, moving image of the embryo she is carrying can be distressing to a woman who is about to undergo an abortion, Dr. Dorfman noted. She stressed that the screen should be turned away from the patient.[16]

A magazine that serves ob-gyns has a physician arguing that the doctor's job is this: *don't allow the woman to see the truth that what's inside her is a baby!*

The Right To Remain Ignorant

When a pro-life candidate ran television ads showing aborted babies, people were outraged.[17] That night, I heard a *CBS Evening News* reporter declare that the abortion debate had reached a "new low in tastelessness." Strangely, there was no outrage that babies were being killed . . . only that someone had the audacity to *show* they were being killed.

The question we should *not* ask is "Why are pro-life people showing these pictures?" (The obvious response is *because the truth matters.*) The question we *should* ask is, "Why would anyone defend what's shown in these pictures?"

The real concern about pictures of unborn babies isn't that they're gory. The concern is that they prove the accuracy of the pro-life position—in abortion, babies die horrible deaths.

In February 2012 Joyce Behar and Barbara Walters, stars of the popular program *The View*, responded to a Texas judge's decision to uphold a law requiring that women look at an ultrasound before having an abortion.

> Joy Behar: It's very totalitarian in my opinion. I mean, it smacks of forcing somebody to confront something that they have already decided they don't want to deal with.

> Barbara Walters: I think that in order to even think about having an abortion, to give up a child that is obviously unwanted, that's why you're doing it, it is such a tremendous decision, it's involved with so much fear of what you're doing and guilt.
>
> Then to have to go and be forced to hear, to see the fetus, to hear the heartbeat, to put more guilt on you, I think is heartbreaking.[18]

Consider this assessment in the clear light of day. A physician being required to inform a woman of the true nature of a medical procedure is "totalitarian" and "heartbreaking"?

Intrauterine photos and ultrasounds aren't hideous, but beautiful and fascinating. So do pro-choice advocates welcome *these* pictures? No. Abortion rights organizations have referred to ultrasound images as a "weapon" in the hand of the pro-life movement.[19]

Pro-choice sociologist Lynn Morgan charges such images originate with "fetus obsessed Americans." In a PBS discussion, one panelist claimed that such pictures reflected "an unhealthy preoccupation with the baby." Notice the terminology: "the baby." Ultrasound technologies are dismantling the age-old pro-choice argument, "It isn't a baby." People are saying, "What are you talking about? *Of course* it's a baby—just *look!*"

Overcoming Denial

The Holocaust was so evil that words alone couldn't describe it. Descriptions of Nazi death camps had long been published in American newspapers, but when these papers started printing the pictures of slaughtered people, the American public finally woke up. If not for the pictures, even today most of us wouldn't understand or believe the Holocaust.

I visited a college campus where a pro-life group set up displays of aborted babies alongside pictures of victims of the Nazi death camps, the killing fields, American slavery, and other historical atrocities. Signs with warnings about the graphic photographs were posted clearly so all those who looked did so by choice. I witnessed the profound silencing effect on students and faculty, including those who didn't want to believe what they were seeing.

According to bioethicist Gregg Cunningham,

Injustice that is invisible
   inevitably becomes tolerable.
But injustice that is made visible
   inevitably becomes intolerable.[20]

Time To Get Off The Fence

There are those who know abortion kills children but have hardened their hearts so much that they may never change, regardless of the facts. But I believe that if most people who are on the fence with the abortion issue—and that's about half of Americans—would force themselves to look at the pictures, they would get off the fence.

Lynn Morgan states that she finds the way pro-life activists use images of the unborn disturbing. She writes, "The images could only be captivating to an audience that accepts and believes in a biological origin story that invests enormous importance in microscopic events that occur inside a pregnant woman's womb."[21]

Never mind that no child is microscopic by the time surgical abortions are performed. Pro-choicers such as Morgan who express outrage at photos of children killed by abortion are betraying their own inner fear and revulsion. Whether or not they admit it, they get angry at the abortion pictures because they *do* understand that the photos depict the killing of real babies. And their outrage is in being exposed as defending something that's indefensible—child-killing. This is a terrible burden to bear, and outrage and anger is a way of deflecting it by trying to make it someone else's fault. (A better way is admitting the truth and changing your position.)

Was the solution to the Holocaust to ban the disgusting pictures? Or was the solution to end the killing?

If the images that show the killing of children are too horrible to look at, is it possible that what they depict is too horrible to defend?

Is the solution to get rid of pictures of dead babies? Or is it getting rid of what's making the babies dead?

Chapter 7

What Makes a Human Life "Meaningful"?

D r. William Harrison, having performed more than twenty thousand abortions in three decades[1] once argued, "The real issue in the abortion debate today is not when life begins, but is it morally meaningful life."[2] But who determines which lives are meaningful and which aren't? The answer always is that powerful people decide whether weaker people's lives are meaningful.

A Double Standard

Princeton ethics professor Peter Singer wrote, "The life of a fetus is of no greater value than the life of a nonhuman animal at a similar level of rationality, self-consciousness, awareness, capacity to feel, etc."[3] (Parents paying for their children to attend Singer's classes might like to know that he also believes there's moral justification for killing the elderly.[4])

A Portland, Oregon, abortionist, Jim Newhall, said, "Not everybody is meant to be born. I believe, for a baby, life begins when his mother wants him."[5] So a human life becomes real only when and if another person values it?

In the 1973 *Roe v. Wade* decision the Supreme Court questioned whether the unborn had "meaningful" lives. But *meaningful to whom?* Doesn't every human being regard as meaningful the life he had in the womb, since if he had been aborted, he would not now be alive?

Read history. Whites once decided that blacks were less human. Men decided women had fewer rights. Nazis decided Jews' lives weren't meaningful. Now big people have decided that little people aren't meaningful enough to have rights.

Personhood isn't something to be bestowed on human beings by Ivy League professors intent on ridding society of "undesirables." Personhood has an inherent value that comes from being a member of the human race. According to the Bible, this is part of being created in God's image.

Viability

In *Roe v. Wade,* the Supreme Court defined viability as the point when the unborn is "potentially able to live outside the mother's womb, albeit with artificial aid."[6] The critical issue in when this point is reached is the development of the child's lungs.

But why make worthiness to live dependent upon the development of the child's lungs? Why not say he becomes human in the fourth week because that's when his heart beats? Or the sixth week because that's when he has brain waves? (Both are also arbitrary yet both would eliminate all abortions currently performed.) Someone could argue that personhood begins when the unborn first sucks his thumb or responds to light and noise. Or why not say that personhood begins when the child takes his first step or is potty trained?

Viability depends not only on the child but on the ability of our technology to save his life. What will happen when we are able to save lives at fifteen weeks or less? Will those children suddenly become human and worthy to live? Can we honestly believe that two decades ago children at twenty-one weeks were not human, but are human now simply because of improved technology? Or can we believe that the unborn at eighteen weeks, who is just barely nonviable, is not a human being, but ten years from now a child at eighteen weeks will be human because hospitals will have better equipment?

Does the baby's nature and worth also depend on which hospital—or country—he is in since some hospitals are equipped to save a nineteen-week-old child and others could save a child no earlier than twenty-eight weeks? Technologies change; babies do not. Surely we cannot believe that the sophistication of life-support systems determines the reality or worth of human life!

In February 2012 an Alabama Supreme Court justice argued in favor of a woman who sued her doctors for wrongful death when her baby died in the womb while only three months in gestation. His position was that the viability standard used in *Roe v. Wade* should be abandoned due to medical breakthroughs—backed by case law and legislation—that have shown a fetus is only as viable as the technology monitoring it.[7]

There is only one objective point of origin for any human being—only one point at which there was not a human being a moment ago, and there is now. That point is conception.

What Science Says of "Meaning"

What constitutes "meaningful" life? It's a scientific fact that there are thought processes at work in unborn babies. The Associated Press reported a study showing "babies start learning about their language-to-be before they are born." While in their mothers' wombs, "fetuses heard, perceived, listened and learned something about the acoustic structure of American English."[8]

This fact and more have been affirmed in later studies as well,[9] so that experts in prenatal development urge that "parenting" should intentionally begin at conception.[10]

As early as 1991, *Newsweek* reported, "Life in the womb represents the next frontier for studies of human development, and the early explorations of the frontier . . . have yielded startling discoveries."[11] The article goes on to say, "With no hype at all, the fetus can rightly be called a marvel of cognition, consciousness and sentience." Decades ago scientists had already detected sentience (self-awareness) in the child's second trimester.[12] The extraordinary capacities of preborn children have been well documented by scientific studies going back to the 70s and early 80s.

By early in the second trimester, the baby moves his hands to shield his eyes from bright light coming in through his mother's body. "The fetus also responds to sounds in frequencies so high or low that they cannot be heard by the human adult ear."[13] He hears high volume music and covers his ears at loud noises from the outside world.

More recent research demonstrates that "The brain of the developing embryo appears to cycle every 20 to 40 minutes between REM sleep, in which brain activity rivals that of consciousness, and non-REM sleep, in which the brain rests."[14]

Can we really say that the same unborn child capable of dreaming is incapable of thinking?

By the end of the second trimester studies demonstrate that the "brain's neural circuits are as advanced as a newborn's."[15]

Yet it is legal to kill that second trimester child—a sentient, thinking human being—for another three months! (Of course, he is still a child even when his neural circuits are *not* yet as advanced as a newborn's.)

It seems unthinkable that anyone aware of the facts of prenatal development could defend the current legality of abortions in the second and third trimesters. Yet pro-choice advocates adamantly defend such abortions.[16]

Even in the case of early chemical abortions, which take life before there's capacity for thought, death is just as real and significant. A living child who would have had a name, family, and life will now have none of these.

Surely the problem of ending the lives of unborn children cannot be solved by simply ending their lives earlier. Rather, it can only be solved by not ending their lives at all.

A Flawed Ethic

Professor Singer says, "If we compare a severely defective human infant with a nonhuman animal, a dog or a pig, for example, we will often find the nonhuman to have superior capacities, both actual and potential, for rationality, self-consciousness, communication and anything else that can plausibly be considered morally significant."[17]

He suggests that individual human worth is based on its usefulness to others: "When the death of a disabled infant will lead to the birth of another infant with better prospects of a happy life, the total amount of happiness will be greater if the disabled infant is killed. The loss of happy life for the first infant is outweighed by the gain of a happier life for the second. Therefore, if killing the hemophiliac infant has no adverse effect on others, it would, according to the total view, be right to kill him."[18]

When Singer first came to teach at Princeton, he was protested by Not Dead Yet, a disabilities rights group. They took offense at Singer's books, which say it should be legal to kill disabled infants, as well as children and adults with severe cognitive disabilities.

Pro-choice logic started with abortion but it hasn't stopped there. Once it's acceptable to kill unborn children, no one who's weak or vulnerable can be safe. Does the handicapped person have a meaningful life? How about the elderly? If those who cannot think don't deserve to live, what about those who think incorrectly?

Dr. Charles Hartshorne of the University of Texas echoes Singer's ethic: "Of course, an infant is not fully human. . . . I have little sympathy with the idea that infanticide is just another form of murder. Persons who are already functionally persons in the full sense have more important rights even than infants."[19]

Is Anyone Safe?

Ethics professor David Boonin argues that abortion is "morally criticizable" yet "morally permissible." It's permissible, he says, because abortion may potentially produce "overall happiness."[20] Like Singer, Boonin ignores the fact that the same subjective sense of happiness (as measured by convenience and relief of stress or financial hardship) can be achieved by taking the lives of other people, not just the unborn. Once something is regarded as morally permissible because it may appear to produce happiness, there's nothing that can't qualify.

In 2012 two ethicists wrote an article for the *Journal of Medical Ethics* arguing that abortion should be allowed on newborns as "not persons." They wrote that "circumstances occur[ing] after birth such that they would have justified abortion, what we call after-birth abortion should be permissible." The authors claim that "both a fetus and a newborn certainly are human beings and potential persons, but neither is a 'person' in the sense of 'subject of a moral right to life.'" [21] Hidden beneath much of the discussion of what constitutes meaningful life is a philosophy of utilitarianism. Are mentally and physically disabled or disadvantaged people useful to the healthy and powerful, or are they a burden to us? And if a burden, do they have an obligation to die?[22]

As one feminist group points out, if unborn children are not safe, no one is safe:

> If we take any living member of the species *Homo sapiens* and put them outside the realm of legal protection, we undercut the case against discrimination for everyone else. The basis for equal treatment under the law is that being a member of the species is sufficient to be a member of the human community, without consideration for race, gender, disability, age, stage of development, state of dependency, place of residence or amount of property ownership.[23]

Having endorsed abortion as a means of decreasing the number of young, will society eventually be tempted to use euthanasia as a means of reducing the old?[24] If back in 1984 the governor of Colorado, looking at the financial costs of longer life, could tell old people they have a "duty to die,"[25] what will happen by the year 2024 when relatively small numbers of taxpayers (a far smaller number due to abortions) will be responsible to pay for the medical care of a large number of the retired? If the elderly don't step aside, will society begin setting them aside?

Who Will Be Next?

In 1985 Surgeon General C. Everett Koop publicly stated his fear that mandatory euthanasia would eventually result from the unwillingness of the younger generation to support the elderly. A Bloomington, Indiana, baby with Down syndrome, widely called "Baby Doe," was denied routine lifesaving surgery by his parents, knowing it would result in the baby's death, which it did. Koop said, "My fear is that one day for every Baby Doe in America, there will be ten thousand Grandma Does."[26]

If the powerful people in a society can strip legal rights from the very young, would it be surprising to see them strip rights from the very old and sick and weak and . . . "useless"?

How twisted is a society that grants the disabled special parking spaces, then declines to feed or give them water when they are in a hospital bed, no longer productive?

Abortion has set us on a dangerous course. We may come to our senses and back away from the slippery slope. Or we may follow it to its inescapable conclusion, becoming a society in which the powerful, for their own self-interest, determine which human beings will live and which will die.

University of Chicago biologist Dr. Leon Kass says concerning the direction of modern science and medicine, "We are already witnessing the erosion of our idea of man as something splendid or divine, as a creature with freedom and dignity. And clearly, if we come to see ourselves as meat, then meat we shall become."[27]

This is the world being shaped by the rhetoric of the abortion rights movement. Is it the world you want your children and your grandchildren to live in?

THE
WOMAN

Chapter 8

Is Abortion Really a Women's Rights Issue?

Kate Michelman, former president of NARAL (National Abortion Rights Action League), said: "We have to remind people that abortion is the guarantor of a woman's . . . right to participate fully in the social and political life of society."[1] But the largely forgotten truth is that early suffragettes were utterly opposed to abortion. Susan B. Anthony called aborting the unborn "child murder."[2]

Killing innocent human beings has never been considered a human right in any civilized society. A pregnant woman *can* fully participate in this society. And if she can't, isn't the solution changing society rather than telling her she can help her cause by killing her children?

How can women achieve equality without control of their reproductive lives? Feminists for Life, a group devoted both to women's rights and the right of the unborn to live, responds this way:

> The premise of the question is the premise of male domination throughout the millennia—that it was nature which made men superior and women inferior. Medical technology is offered as a solution to achieve equality; but the premise is wrong. . . . It's an insult to women to say women must change their biology in order to fit into society.[3]

Pregnancy Is Not An Illness

In her essay "Feminism: Bewitched by Abortion," environmentalist Rosemary Bottcher argues that the feminist movement has degraded women by portraying them as unable to handle the stress and pressures of pregnancy without resorting to killing their children.[4]

In spite of a woman's reproductive capacity and the record of human history in which pregnancy is a normative stressor, pro-choice advocates and the Supreme Court choose to view pregnancy as an illness. Legalizing abortion implies that pregnancy is now so traumatic that it poses a significant risk to a woman's life.

There is heated debate about whether health care should cover abortions, and whether employers whose consciences forbid supporting abortion would be required to do so by providing health care programs that cover abortions.

But the most striking aspect of this discussion is that abortion, killing a child, is treated as though it were equivalent to the surgical removal of a cancer. Pregnancy is not a disease. A child is not a tumor. Abortion is not health care.

All the Risk, None of the Accountability

It is remarkable that abortion is given special treatment under the law. Pro-choice groups consistently oppose efforts to require that abortion be treated like every other surgery when it comes to informing the patient of its nature and risks. They don't seem to believe that women are capable of making intelligent choices when presented with the facts.

To most pro-choice advocates, even the simple requirement of "informed consent" is threatening. Pro-choice activist and blogger A. B. Stevens, reacting against such legislation, writes, "This language of 'informed consent' merely serves as a thinly veiled attempt at shaming women who seek abortion."[5]

Is abortion really about serving and empowering women, or is it about something else? Doesn't it assume the worst of women, that they would be unable to handle hearing the results of studies that demonstrate the medical risks of abortion and the facts about their unborn child's development?

Why do pro-choice advocates appear not to care that by refusing to tell women these facts, one day—months or years after an abortion—women will come to understand what was true all along? They will wonder then what I have heard women ask again and again: *"Why did no one tell me the truth when I still had a chance to choose?"*

Abortion as Commerce

Planned Parenthood Federation's 2009–2010 financial statement reported profits that exceeded $1 billion. Taxpayers supplied an astounding 46% of that revenue.[6] Pro-choice groups rarely point out that they have obtained $460 million in government revenue from taxpayers, many of whom are morally opposed to that industry.

Pro-life activist Lila Rose and a film crew captured Planned Parenthood staff promoting the revenue end of abortion on camera on several occasions.[7] In one "sting" reported on January 13, 2011, by CBS and ABC News, a New Jersey Planned Parenthood manager offered to cooperate in illegal sex-trafficking to provide abortion services for underage, non-English-speaking girls, who had presumably been kidnapped. The couple being counseled was, as far as the staff person knew, a pimp and one of his partners.[8]

Planned Parenthood alone spent more than $1 million to support pro-choice candidates in 2010, which wasn't a heavy election year. They paid lobbyists more than six hundred thousand dollars to promote their industry that same year.

In the midst of a debate on increasing the national debt ceiling to operate the federal government, in April 2011 Planned Parenthood sent out a letter to media outlets carefully warning them against reporting the deadlock as due to arguments over "abortion funding." National Public Radio (NPR) posted the letter which reads in part:

> A number of outlets have reported that the standoff on Capitol Hill concerns "abortion funding." This is wholly inaccurate and is nothing more than a political talking point. . . .
>
> It is not a proposal over funding for abortion but a debate over a proposal to exclude [Planned Parenthood] . . . from participating in existing federal programs.[9]

Planned Parenthood states over 90 percent of their services are not abortion-related, but their annual report demonstrates that 329,445 abortions were performed and accounted for 91 percent of their services.[10] This makes Planned Parenthood by far the largest abortion provider in America.

"Planned Parenthood's new use of Skype to dispense abortion-inducing drugs and its mandate that all affiliates provide abortion services by 2013 also indicate that the organization wants its abortion-increasing trend to continue."[11]

Serrin Foster, president of Feminists for Life, says that historically the primary activists against abortion were women. She says, "Without known exception, the early American feminists condemned abortion in the strongest possible terms."[12]

Early Pro-Life Feminists

Susan B. Anthony stood for women's rights at a time when women weren't allowed to vote. Anthony saw abortion as a means of exploiting both women and children. She wrote, "I deplore the horrible crime of child murder. . . . No matter what the motive, love of ease, or a desire to save from suffering the unborn innocent, the woman is awfully guilty who commits the deed."[13] Her newspaper, *The Revolution,* argued, "When a woman destroys the life of her unborn child, it is a sign that, by education or circumstances, she has been greatly wronged."[14]

Alice Paul, who wrote the original version of the Equal Rights Amendment (ERA), a landmark feminist document, referred to abortion as "the ultimate exploitation of women."[15] Yet abortion advocates have consistently tried to establish abortion as a fundamental right by framing it within the ERA.[16] That the woman who drafted the ERA in the first place opposed legalized abortion demonstrates how inappropriate it is to confuse or combine women's rights with the right to kill unborn children.

Planned Parenthood's Founder

Anthony, Paul, and other feminists who opposed abortion were followed later by a new breed. Most prominent was Margaret Sanger who advocated not only contraception, but abortion as a means of eugenics,[17] economics, and sexual liberation.

Margaret Sanger was the direction-setter and first president of Planned Parenthood, the world's largest abortion promoter and provider. The shocking truth, which I have carefully researched, is that her organization viewed abortion as one more means of controlling the birthrate of those they considered inferior.

I have in front of me a stack of Sanger's original writings, as well as copies of her magazine, *Birth Control Review*. I encourage readers to read these writings and discover the beliefs and attitudes that gave birth to Planned Parenthood and the American abortion movement.[18] (Some quotations attributed to Margaret Sanger in pro-life sources are inaccurate, or at least the citations are inaccurate. Since I have not located these statements in any original documents, I can only assume that they are not authentic. Citations from Sanger and the *Birth Control Review* in this edition are limited to quotations from copies of original documents in my possession.)

Margaret Sanger spoke of the poor and handicapped as the "sinister forces of the hordes of irresponsibility and imbecility," claiming their existence constituted an "attack upon the stocks of intelligence and racial health."[19] She warned of "indiscriminate breeding" among the less fit that would bring into the world future voters "who may destroy our liberties, and who may thus be the most far-reaching peril to the future of civilization."[20] She called the less privileged members of society "a dead weight of human waste."[21]

In a chapter called the "Cruelty of Charity," Sanger argued that groups dedicated to helping pregnant women decide to give birth to their children were "positively injurious to the community and the future of the race."[22] She claimed, "The effect of maternity endowments and maternity centers supported by private philanthropy would have, perhaps already have had, exactly the most dysgenic tendency."[23] Her use of the technical term *dysgenic* clearly indicates her belief that these woman-helping efforts violated Darwin's doctrine of the survival of the fittest, by which the weaker were naturally eliminated by virtue of their inferiority.

This same spirit permeates Sanger's magazine, *Birth Control Review*. It is full of articles with titles such as "The World's Racial Problem," "Toward Race Betterment," and "Eugenic Sterilization: An Urgent Need."[24] The latter article was written in 1933 by Dr. Ernst Rudin, a leader in the German eugenics movement that was busily laying the foundation for the Nazis' acts of "racial improvement" and "ethnic cleansing."

Sanger, Planned Parenthood, and Eugenics

The international eugenics movement, of which Margaret Sanger was definitely a part, was openly praising Nazi racial policies at least as late as 1938.[25] Sanger gave the welcoming address to a 1925 international eugenics conference.[26]

According to writer Marvin Olasky, Margaret Sanger's "Negro Project" of the 1930s was "hailed for its work in spreading contraception among those whom eugenicists most deeply feared."[27] When it became evident that contraceptives were not sufficiently curtailing the black population and other target groups, the eugenicists turned to abortion as a solution to the spread of unwanted races and families.[28]

In Margaret Sanger's own words, to help the weaker and less privileged survive and to allow them to reproduce was to take a step backward in human evolution: "Instead of decreasing and aiming to eliminate the stocks that are most detrimental to the future of the race and the world, it tends to render them to a menacing degree dominant."[29]

These "stocks" were the poor and uneducated, a large portion of whom were ethnic minorities. Sanger was more interested in "aiming to eliminate" these "stocks" (read *people*) than in helping them.

This history helps to explain why to this day Planned Parenthood does virtually nothing to promote adoption or help poor and minority women who choose to give their children life rather than abort them. Planned Parenthood has even brought legal action to shut down pregnancy centers that give women other choices besides abortion.

Though I have read many Planned Parenthood materials, I have never seen any that renounce or apologize for Sanger's blatant eugenicism, her bias against the poor and the mentally and physically handicapped, and her racism, all of which characterized Planned

Parenthood's philosophy from its inception. That some highly visible minority leaders work for Planned Parenthood does not change its heritage or philosophy.

I do not believe most people who support abortion rights are racists, nor do I believe there are no racists among pro-lifers. I do believe that regardless of motives, a closer look at both the history and present strategies of the pro-choice movement suggests that abortion for the minorities may not serve the cause of racial equality nearly as much as the cause of upper-class white supremacy.

Abortion and Women's Rights Today

One of Sanger's early stated goals was to promote "Unlimited sexual gratification without the burden of unwanted children."[30]

Following the Holocaust, eugenics (of which abortion was one part) fell into disfavor. Sanger's organization went underground. Later it resurfaced as the Planned Parenthood Federation.[31]

Former abortionist Dr. Bernard Nathanson stated that in the 1960s, he and his fellow abortion-rights strategists deliberately linked abortion to the women's issue so it could be furthered not on its own merits but on the merits of women's rights.[32]

One feminist argues that the attempt to marry feminism to abortion is a form of "terrorist feminism." In her words, it forces the feminist to be "willing to kill for the cause you believe in."[33]

In their publication *The American Feminist,* Feminists for Life features the beautiful face of a child and asks, "Is this the face of the enemy?" They argue that they stand on two hundred years of pro-life feminist history, and that it wasn't until the 1970s that the larger women's movement finally embraced abortion.[34]

In the past, polls have indicated that more women than men affirm the unborn's right to life.[35] At one time "the most pro-abortion category in the United States (and also in other nations) [was] white males between the ages of twenty and forty-five."[36] More specifically, "the group that is most consistently pro-choice is actually single men."[37]

It's ironic that abortion has been turned into a women's rights issue when it has encouraged male irresponsibility and failure to care for women and children. Shouldn't men be called upon to do more than just provide money to kill their children? Shouldn't they be encouraged instead to say to the woman they've made pregnant, "I'll be there for our child. I'll do everything I can for her. And if you're willing to have me, I'll be there for you too."

Anti-Woman Sex Selection

One of the ironies of feminism is that by its advocacy of abortion, it has endorsed the single greatest means of robbing women of their most basic right—the right to life.

According to an ABC News story aired in December 2011, the pressure on women in India to provide male offspring has resulted in an estimated fifty thousand girls being aborted each month; over a million each year.[38] As a result, males outnumber females by forty million. Even making ultrasound technology for the use of sex-selection unlawful has not succeeded; underground ultrasound clinics operate to get around the law.[39]

In the United States, Dr. Sunita Puri, serving an Indian immigrant population, wanted to find out why many of her patients were eager to know the sex of the child they were carrying. Over the course of sixty-five interviews she discovered "89 percent of the women carrying girls opted for an abortion, and nearly half had previously aborted girls." Another shock was that the choice to abort girls was not based on "free-will," but often involved violence within the family in order to "coerce them into aborting."[40]

A paper presented to the National Academy of Sciences says an estimated eighty million females were aborted in China and India alone.[41] The same gendercide-by-ultrasound is practiced throughout Asia.[42]

Worldwide Abortion as Sex Selection

Britain's *The Telegraph* reported in January 2012 that more women in that country are using "selective reduction," having an abortion targeting one or more children for death in order to leave only one survivor when a pregnancy has resulted in twins or triplets.[43] At the same time the National Health Service (NHS) warns that such "reductions" pose a danger to the baby the woman "wants" to remain alive.

> Mothers-to-be should be given information on the "physical risks and psychological implications" of what is known as "selective fetal reduction" before their fetuses are screened for Down syndrome.
>
> [The warning] comes as increasing numbers of women choose to abort one of their twins or triplets, usually because of the risk that they will be born disabled.[44]

This reproductive schizophrenia is even more apparent as we consider a third news story (all of these published on the same day): While some researchers work feverishly to eliminate children, in Germany and Israel scientists are learning how to grow sperm in the lab so that men incapable of fathering a child will be able, in the future, to participate in designer children.[45] The only one left without options is the small individual that society, doctors, and parents choose either to let live or die.

In December 2011 a United Nations Family Planning report expressed alarm that Armenian women too are having abortions based upon a six-to-one desire to value boys over girls. The report states, "This means that each year Armenia potentially loses around 1400 future mothers."[46]

Dr. Stephen Mosher, an expert on demographics in China, discovered "son-biased sex ratios" at birth among US-born children of Chinese, Korean, and Asian-Indian parents. They found that for every 151 boys, there were only 100 surviving girls. The rest of the girls were killed by abortion.[47]

Abortion has become the primary means of eliminating unwanted females across the globe, but it is not new. In 1989 a survey of a dozen villages in India uncovered a frightening statistic: out of a total population of ten thousand, only fifty were girls.[48] The other girls, thousands of them, had been killed by abortion. In Bombay, of eight thousand amniocentesis tests indicating the babies were female, all but one of the girls were killed by abortion.[49]

Because of sex-selection abortions, two-thirds of children born in China are now males. In the countryside, the ratio of boys to girls is four to one.[50] One journal reports that the Chinese male population under twenty years old exceeds the female population by thirty-two million as of 2009. Why? Abortion and the preference for a male over a female.

Amniocentesis is also used to detect a child's gender in America. As early as 1975, *Medical World News* reported a study in which ninety-nine mothers were informed of the sex of their children. Fifty-three of these preborns were boys and forty-six were girls. Only one mother elected to abort her boy, while twenty-nine elected to abort their girls.[51] Every report I have ever seen shows that when the gender is known, far more parents will choose to abort girls than boys.

So how do pro-choice feminists respond to this targeted killing of unborn females? According to the journal *BioEthics*, "Any prohibition of the use of this technology is a curtailment of a woman's reproductive choices and a violation of her right to make autonomous decisions regarding procreation."[52]

They seem unconcerned that the influence of future *born* women will be diminished rather than enhanced simply because males will so greatly outnumber females in many countries around the world.

To kill an unborn female is to kill a young woman. *There can be no equal rights for all women until there are equal rights for unborn women.*

Chapter 9

Do We Have the Right to Choose What We Do with Our Bodies?

Pro-choice advocates argue, "Every woman has the right to choose what she does with her own body." Ironically the choice of abortion assures that something like 650,000 females in the United States each year don't have the right to choose what they do with *their* bodies. (That number is roughly half of aborted children, the other half being males, though as we've seen the rate of females aborted is even higher.)

The fact is that a female killed by abortion no longer has a life, a choice, or a body to exercise control over. All these have been stripped from her by adults.

Despite the fact that he is choosing to do what he wants to with his own body, a man isn't legally permitted to expose himself. There are laws against public urination, prostitution, drug use, trespassing, and even loitering, even though every one of them involves a choice to do something with one's own body. Most of us agree with these laws, even though they restrict personal freedoms, but always in the interests of others whose personal freedoms they directly or indirectly violate.

My hand is part of my body, but I'm not free to use it to strike you or steal from you or hurt your child—or mine. *Aren't you glad the law prevents me from doing whatever I might want with my own body?*

The Right to Choose

When presenting the pro-life position on public school campuses, I've sometimes begun by saying, "I am pro-choice."

Immediately students look relieved. Sometimes they applaud. I go on to say, "And because I am pro-choice, I believe every man has the right to rape a woman if that's his choice. After all, it's his body, and we don't have the right to tell him what he can and cannot do with it."

After I let the shock settle in, I ask them to tell me the fallacy of my argument. They point out that in asserting the man's right to choose *I've ignored the harm done to the innocent woman whose rights have been violated.*

I say, "So you're telling me you're anti-choice?"

After they argue that some choices should be illegal, I ask, "So actually you're pro-choice about some choices and anti-choice about other choices. And it all depends on what the choice is and whether it harms the innocent?"

Yes, they agree.

I respond, "So you're saying that if I can demonstrate to you that a woman's choice to have an abortion harms or kills another human being, then you'll no longer be pro-choice about abortion?"

My hope is that they will heed their own common sense, which is perfectly sound—but which they've failed to apply to abortion.

It's absurd to defend a specific choice simply on the basis that it's a choice. *Every single evil thing that has ever been done by one person to another is a choice.* And every good thing anyone does is also a choice. The fact that something is a choice tells us absolutely nothing about whether or not it should be legal.

The high-sounding "right to choose" ignores the obvious: *not all choices are legitimate,* and no one is uniformly pro-choice or anti-choice.

Selectively Pro-Choice

I confess that I dislike the term *pro-choice.* I use it only because it has become the dominant term used in our culture. But it is profoundly misleading.

When we talk about someone being pro-environment, pro-business, or pro-marijuana, we have a good idea what they mean.

But what if someone insisted we not use the words *environment*, *business,* or *marijuana*? No, we must just call these positions *pro-choice.*

But choice is not a synonym for environment, business, or marijuana. The term *pro-choice* obscures the subject we are talking about, because it demands the explanation, "pro-choice *about what?*" If our attention is on the "right to choose," we can be distracted from the subject at hand.

The term *pro-abortion* tells us that someone thinks abortion is okay. Whether or not they would have one, they favor abortion's legality. Okay, we can agree or disagree, but at least the term tells us what we're talking about.

The term *pro-choice* tells us that someone thinks *choice* is okay. Well, of course. But what does that mean?

All of us are pro-choice when it comes to where people live, what kind of car they drive, what food they eat, and thousands of personal preferences. We're also pro-choice in matters of religion, politics, and lifestyle, even when people choose beliefs and behavior we don't like. Indeed, I am pro-choice about the great majority of things in life, even when I personally don't agree with someone's choice. I have no interest in dictating their choices, nor do I want them dictating mine.

But that's not the end of it, because there are many things almost none of us are pro-choice about—including whether someone has the right to choose to assault you, break into your house, steal your car, or cheat you in a business deal.

Of course, it's self-evident that people have the *freedom* to make these choices. But that doesn't mean they have the *right* to make them.

What would you think of someone who said, "I wouldn't rob you myself, but I am pro-choice about robbery."

Well, not only would we say they are wrong to defend robbery, we would not allow them to hijack the term *pro-choice* as their means of taking the moral high ground. We would say, "Stop talking about *choice*—the issue is robbery! You are not pro-choice, you are pro-robbery!"

Pro-Choice or Pro-Abortion?

In discussing abortion with pro-choice people, I sometimes de-liberately use the term *pro-abortion*. Inevitably they react against it, sometimes very defensively. They say, "I am *not* pro-abortion, I am pro-choice!" Clearly they feel insulted. Then I ask, "What is it about abortion that's so bad you don't want to be known as pro-abortion?"

The answer is that the word *choice* successfully changes the sub-ject, while the word *abortion* doesn't. The old terms *anti-abortion* and *pro-abortion* were more accurate and less confusing than the modern terms *pro-life* and *pro-choice*. Increasing numbers of people hijack the term *pro-life* to argue against capital punishment or just war, or to defend select groups of already-born people. Some are now calling themselves "pro-life" who actually consent to legal abortion, priding themselves that they advocate justice for other oppressed and vulnerable people, while ignoring the rights of pre-born children.

The term *pro-choice* is worse, in that it entirely shifts the abor-tion issue away from abortion itself. It attempts to take the moral high ground, as if it would be cruel to rob people of a "right" no one should have—to kill innocent preborn children.

Both terms, by avoiding the word *abortion*, can obscure what's at stake—an innocent preborn child's right to live.

From a propaganda point of view, I must admit that the pro-abortion movement has won the battle of semantics. *Choice* has become a euphemism for abortion that veils abortion's horrors. Arguing against abortion *appears* to be arguing against choice.

Pro-lifers must never argue against choice—that's a battle that can't be won, and shouldn't be fought even if it could be won. Rather, we must argue against the real issue—*abortion*.

Whenever we hear "pro-choice," we must ask, and urge others to ask, "*Exactly what choice are we talking about?*"

If it's abortion, the question is, "*Do you think people should have the right to choose to kill children?*" By opposing abortion we are not opposing choice in general. We are opposing *one choice* in particular—child-killing.

Consider the popular pro-choice question, which I've seen on bumper stickers: "If you don't trust me with a choice, how can you trust me with a child?" It's intended as a discussion stopper. But notice how *choice* is substituted for *abortion*. When we insert words that reflect reality, the question becomes, "If you don't trust me to kill a child, how can you trust me to raise a child?" . . . Huh?

When we oppose the "right to choose" rape or "the right to choose" abortion, we aren't opposing a *right*. Rather, we're opposing a *wrong*. And we're not narrow-minded and bigoted for doing so.

A Civil Rights Issue

Martin Luther King, Jr., said, in words prominently displayed on Portland's Justice Center, "Injustice anywhere is a threat to justice everywhere." The daily stories of people killing already-born children are shocking. But these are simply a logical extension of the abortion mentality. If a parent has the right to take a child's life six months before birth, why not six months after? Same parent. Same child. Other than size and age, what's the difference?

We must oppose abortion for the same reason we oppose slavery—it is a fundamental violation of human rights. There is no God-given right to convenience, but there is a God-given right to life. The concentration camps of Nazi Germany are a testimony to what happens when people in power start deciding who has the right to live and who doesn't. The sign at Auschwitz says "Never Again." Yet holocausts have happened again. I hope that someday our country will admit that abortion kills children and will say, "Never Again."

All people are "created equal," not just "born equal." You don't have to have been born to be a person any more than you have to have walked or talked to be a person.

Of course, any two people are equal and have equal rights. Hence, a mother has every bit as much right to live as a child. But in nearly all abortions, the woman's right to live is *not* an issue, because her life is not in danger.

The right to a certain lifestyle is never absolute and unconditional. It is always governed by its effects on others. Planned Parenthood states, "The desire to complete school or to continue working are common reasons women give for choosing to abort an unplanned pregnancy."[1]

Completing school and working are desirable things in many cases. Pregnancy can make them difficult. But a woman normally can continue school and work during pregnancy. If she places her child for adoption, she need not give up school or work. If she chooses to raise the child herself, there are child care options available if she must work outside the home. There are even laws that allow a woman to anonymously relinquish her child at a hospital or other agency.[2]

Regardless of the challenges, *one person's right to a lifestyle is not greater than another person's right to a life.*

What About the Victim's Choice?

One female points out, "After a woman is pregnant, she cannot choose whether or not she wishes to become a mother. She already is . . . all that is left to her to decide is whether she will deliver her baby dead or alive."[3]

Slave owners were pro-choice. They emphasized physical differences to justify their claim to superiority over the enslaved. They said, "You don't have to own slaves, but don't tell us we can't choose to own slaves." Those who wanted slave-holding to be illegal were accused of being anti-choice and anti-freedom, and imposing their anti-slavery morality on others.[4] The language was eerily similar to what pro-lifers hear constantly.

Every movement of oppression and exploitation—from slavery, to prostitution, to drug dealing, to abortion—has labeled itself pro-choice. Likewise, they've labeled opposing movements that offer compassion and deliverance as "anti-choice."

The pro-choice position is notorious for overlooking the victim's right to choose.

Blacks didn't choose slavery.

Jews didn't choose the ovens.

Women don't choose rape.

Babies don't choose abortion.

Chapter 10

Does Our "Right to Privacy" Include Abortion?

We've all heard it said, "Abortion is no one else's business. Everyone has a right to privacy."

Contrary to popular belief, the US Constitution says nothing about a right to privacy. Of course, we all have a general right to privacy. But privacy is *never* an absolute right. Rather, it is always governed by other and higher rights, which it never trumps.

What would we think of a man who defended wife-beating by saying, "What I do privately is no one's business but mine"? Or a man who said, "Look, if I want to beat up or molest *my* child behind closed doors, on *my* private property, that is none of *your* business!"

Consider the statement, "Abortion is a private decision between a woman and her doctor." Surely the fact that a decision is made privately has no bearing whatsoever on whether it should be legal. A man who hires someone to kill his wife does so privately, but privacy does not legitimize his actions.

Physicians are trained in medicine, but their *moral* opinions aren't as authoritative as their medical diagnoses (which themselves can be flawed). Many doctors are conscientious people who place human welfare above expedience and money. Unfortunately, history demonstrates that doctors, like all people, are capable of practicing and justifying harm to others.[1]

Nazi Doctors

Robert Jay Lifton, in his powerful book *The Nazi Doctors*, documents how intelligent medical professionals participated in cruel and deadly surgeries and experiments on helpless children with shocking ease.[2] They were the best-trained medical personnel in Europe, but they lost their moral compass.

And German doctors weren't alone. During World War II, in the United States and Britain, leading eugenics researchers and charitable foundations funded and promoted racist organizations targeting Jews and the handicapped.[3] Educated men around the globe justified doing horrible things in their home countries, all under the guise that they were acting as objective scientists.

Doctors who perform abortions are no more objective about abortion than researchers for tobacco companies are objective about cigarette smoking. Their personal and financial vested interests in their respective trades, as well as the desensitization of their consciences, disqualify them as sources of moral guidance.

Wisdom From Experience

Many young women and their parents don't want to be embarrassed in front of critical onlookers. They may have vested interests in a false "right to privacy."

But regardless of anyone's opinion about sex outside of marriage, pregnancy is not wrong, even if the act that resulted in pregnancy was. No one should treat the mother as a "bad girl," or pressure her to "solve her problem" by aborting her child. We should love her and support her through the pregnancy, offering her guidance as to whether to raise the child or choose adoption.

Whenever I see an unmarried woman carrying a child, my first response is appreciation. I realize she could have taken the "quick fix" of abortion without anyone knowing, but she chose instead to let her child live.

Premarital sex has serious consequences even apart from unwanted pregnancy. For this reason we should enthusiastically endorse abstinence education.[4] Abstinence is saying no to what harms you, and in doing so it's saying yes to the life that's best for you. But after it's happened, premarital sex can be learned from and not repeated.

Killing an innocent human being by abortion is both more serious and more permanently debilitating than the choices that preceded it. It makes one person pay with their life for another's mistake. Abortion may temporarily hide a problem, but it never solves it.

Abortion fosters the attitude, "My comfort and happiness come first—even if I have to disregard the rights of an innocent person to get them." This attitude emerges in a thousand other arenas, big and small, which cumulatively tear apart the moral fabric of society. (And, ironically, it never delivers the happiness it promises.)

Even when pregnancy is unwanted or difficult, it is a temporary condition. Contrary to popular belief, abortion doesn't save a woman from nine months of inconvenience. Usually from the time a woman knows she is pregnant until her natural delivery is between six and seven months. The time until her child would be viable if she had a premature delivery is four or five months, half of a pregnancy's normal duration.

I have heard pro-choice advocates speak of a woman being "chained" to her child for many years. But after birth a woman is free to place her child with one of the 1.3 million US families waiting to adopt infants in this country. While pregnancy is a temporary condition, abortion produces a permanent condition—the death of a child. One person's temporarily difficult circumstances do not justify taking the life of another person.

The Father's Rights and Responsibilities

On the one hand, a man is told he should take responsibility for an unwanted pregnancy and give the child's mother financial help and emotional support.

On the other hand, if the same child he's responsible to love and support is to be aborted, the man is told that abortion is none of his business, but only the mother's. Given this mixed message, why should we expect men to act responsibly toward the mother and child?

Ironically, abortion allows and even encourages men to sexually exploit women without the fear of having to take responsibility for any children conceived. If the woman does get pregnant, the man can hand over three hundred dollars and buy a dead child. When the man is long gone, with no child to love and support, the woman is left with the burden of having killed her child.

"Abortion rights" brings out the worst in men.

The implication of the "just between a mother and her doctor" argument is that no one else will have to deal with the consequences of the decision. On the contrary, abortion has powerful long-term effects on men.

Men Speak Out

In an *Esquire* magazine article, twelve men speak candidly on the price they have paid because of abortion.[5] Some agreed to the decision to abort, some didn't. Some pushed the decision to abort, but now desperately wish they hadn't:

> It's her body, but I had her brainwashed. I made all the decisions. Once it was over, we never talked about it again. We kept our mouths shut. She did have some real prophetic words, though. She said, "Wagner, you're going to regret this all your life." I told her, "No, no." But inside me something would spark and cling to that. She was right. I'll never forget it. I'll never forgive myself.

A married man reflects:

> We tried to figure out why we weren't getting along so well. It occurred to one of us that it was a year since the abortion. That was the first time we realized that we felt we had killed something that we had made together and that it would have been alive and might have been our child. . . . We talked and shared how disturbed about it we both had been. . . . We hadn't known that we were angry and upset and hadn't been willing to face the facts.

One man reluctantly agreed to an abortion. Years later he said:

> I've got to think of the pain and the damage it did to her, because I know about the pain that it does to me, and it wasn't my decision. I was part of the cause and I certainly didn't resist in any way. I can't help but think, am I guilty of being an accomplice in the taking of a life, or at least in not bringing it to fruition? There's guilt, but more than anything, there's just sadness.

Another man demonstrates an understanding that not only women, but many men come to years after an abortion:

I've had a hell of a time dealing with it, actually . . . I've come to believe more and more that the baby in the womb is just that—a human life. I wish I didn't. I wish I could make myself believe differently, but I can't. It would make it easier to deal with mentally. When you have the opposite view and you go through with the abortion anyway, well, that's worse than anything.

So, you see, I'm kind of stuck. She did it for me. I feel like I murdered somebody. I wish I could do it over again, if I could just go back in time and relive those years. If she'd had the child, even if we'd got married and everything, it wouldn't have been that bad. I've seen other people do it. Reality's such a bitch sometimes, you know?

Chapter 11

Does Abortion Harm a Woman's Physical and Mental Health?

A bortion has completely failed as a social policy designed to aid women," writes Serrin Foster, president of Feminists for Life. "It is a reflection that we have failed women."[1]

Joan Appleton was an abortion advocate with the National Organization of Women (NOW) and head nurse at a Virginia abortion facility. She asked herself why abortion was "such a psychological trauma for a woman. . . . If it was so right, why was it so difficult?"

Appleton thought, "I counseled these women so well; they were so sure of their decision. Why are they coming back now—months and years later—psychological wrecks?"[2]

Karen Sullivan Ables says she wasn't told the truth of what her abortion might do to her:

> I could feel the baby being torn from my insides. It was really painful. . . . Three-quarters of the way through the operation I sat up. . . . In the cylinder I saw the bits and pieces of my little child floating in a pool of blood. I screamed and jumped up off the table. . . . I just couldn't stop throwing up. . . .

> I had nightmares and recurring dreams about my baby. I couldn't work my job. I just lay in my bed and cried. Once, I wept so hard I sprained my ribs. Another time while crying, I was unable to breathe and I passed out. I was unable to walk on the beach because the playing children would make me cry. Even Pampers commercials would set me into fits of uncontrollable crying.[3]

Countless women who have been damaged by abortions have said, "I had no idea this could happen; no one warned me about the risks."

Mental Health Complications

Dr. Patricia Coleman, professor of Human Development and Family Studies at Bowling Green State University, analyzed outcomes of twenty-two scholarly research papers on women, mental health, and abortion. The research involved well over 877,000 women. She states, "81 percent of females who had an abortion were found to be at an increased risk for mental health problems, including depression, alcohol abuse, and suicidal behaviors."[4]

Coleman's meta-analysis, published in *The British Journal of Psychiatry,* was met with a barrage of letters indicating a deep suspicion of her findings. They were subject to rejection because Coleman was found to have an opinion on abortion and a desire to see the research find its way into the mainstream of mental health publications.[5]

In addressing her critics, Coleman pointed to a bias in published research, stating, "In 1969 the APA [American Psychological Association] passed a resolution which made the pro-choice political position the organization's official stance and declared abortion a civil right. . . . Politically motivated efforts to publish null findings to support and legitimize their position is logical."[6]

Very similar conclusions to Coleman's were reached independently in an Australian analysis of abortion and mental health data.[7]

Other Psychological Complications

Over the years, dozens of studies have tied abortion to a rise in sexual dysfunction, aversion to sex, loss of intimacy, unexpected guilt, extramarital affairs, traumatic stress syndrome, personality fragmentation, grief response, child abuse and neglect, and increase in alcohol and drug abuse.[8] An Elliot Institute study indicates that women who abort are five times more likely to abuse drugs.[9]

Post-abortion researcher Dr. David Reardon writes, "In a study of post-abortion patients only eight weeks after their abortion, researchers found that 44 percent complained of nervous disorders, 36 percent had experienced sleep disturbances, 31 percent had regrets about their decision, and 11 percent had been prescribed psychotropic medicine by their family doctor."[10]

This is particularly significant since some women show no apparent effects from their abortions until years later. And while pro-choice advocates are often quick to assert there is no such thing as post-abortion stress syndrome (PASS), others grudgingly acknowledge consequences usually associated with post-traumatic stress disorder (PTSD).[11]

Abortion Support Groups

Since abortion was legalized in 1973, a number of post-abortion help groups have come into existence. Women Exploited by Abortion (WEBA) has had more than thirty thousand members in more than two hundred chapters across the United States, and in Canada, Germany, Ireland, Japan, Australia, New Zealand, and Africa.[12]

Other post-abortion support and recovery groups include Victims of Choice, Post-Abortion Counseling and Education (PACE), Safe Haven, Silent No More, Helping and Educating in Abortion-Related Trauma (HEART), Counseling for Abortion-Related Experiences (CARE), Women of Ramah, Project Rachel, Open Arms, Abortion Trauma Services, American Victims of Abortion, Former Women of Choice, and more. The existence of such groups testifies to the mental and emotional trauma of countless women who have had abortions.

I read a newspaper editorial arguing that abortion is just another surgery, no different from a root canal or appendectomy. But why don't people remember the anniversary of their appendectomy twenty years later? Why don't they find themselves weeping uncontrollably, grieving the loss of their appendix or tonsils? And where are all the support groups and counselors working with those who've had root canals?

(Many men have also suffered trauma due to their involvement in abortion decisions, and the loss of their children.[13] Support groups exist for them as well.[14])

Physical Complications

In her testimony before a Senate subcommittee in 2004, gynecologist and scientist Elizabeth Shadigian testified that "abortion increases rates of breast cancer,[15] placenta previa, preterm births, and maternal suicide. . . . Statistically, all types of deaths are higher with women who have had induced abortions."[16]

Many studies have demonstrated a statistically significant increase in miscarriage, premature births or low birth weight risk in women with prior induced abortions.[17] "Low birth weight and premature birth are the most important risk factors for infant mortality or later disabilities as well as for lower cognitive abilities and greater behavioral problems."[18]

There has been considerable discussion about why black American women have three times more premature births than average. The main reason is likely that black women abort 4.3 times more than non-black women.[19] If these facts are related, then it is not only the children who immediately die in abortion, but also the future siblings who are *not* aborted whose health is adversely affected.

The odds of malformations in later children are also increased by abortion.[20] The frequency of early death for infants born after their mothers have had abortions is between two and four times the normal rate.[21] Because induced abortion increases the risk of delivering a future baby prematurely, it appears to be responsible for thousands of cases of cerebral palsy.[22]

An increase in nonsurgical "medication abortions" using Methotrexate (MTX) or RU-486, have resulted in the presence of harmful agents "during prenatal life that produces permanent physical or functional defect in the offspring." Folic acid deficiencies triggered by MTX result in broken chromosomes, hydrocephalus, Down syndrome, neural-tube defects, complex cardiac malformation, Kleinfelter's syndrome, and a host of other defects.[23]

In a 2012 study focused on the link between gestational diabetes and autism risk, the researchers also reported that prior induced abortions increase the risk of autism in infants.[24]

PID, Placenta Previa, And Cancer

Pelvic Inflammatory Disease (PID) is an infection that leads to fever and infertility. Researchers state, "Pelvic infection is a common and serious complication of induced abortion and has been reported in up to 30 percent of all cases."

A study of women having first-trimester abortions established that "women with post-abortal pelvic inflammatory disease had significantly higher rates of . . . spontaneous abortion, secondary infertility, dyspareunia [painful intercourse], and chronic pelvic pain."[25]

Placenta previa, a misplacement of the placenta, is caused by "prior uterine insult or injury,"[26] including abortion.[27] There is a 70 percent increase in the condition for women who have undergone an induced abortion.[28]

The Guttmacher Institute states that about half of women who have had an abortion will go on to have more.[29] Women with one abortion double their risk of cervical cancer, compared to nonabortive women, while women with two or more abortions multiply their risk by nearly five times. Similar elevated risks of ovarian and liver cancer have also been linked to single and multiple abortions.[30]

After extensive investigation, Dr. Joel Brind, a cancer researcher and professor of endocrinology, concluded, "The single most avoidable risk factor for breast cancer is induced abortion."[31] A woman who has an abortion increases her risk of breast cancer by a minimum of 50 percent and as much as 300 percent.[32]

Following the publication of such research, many pro-choice organizations such as Media Matters for America[33] and research foundations rejected the data.[34] Unfortunately, they have vested interests in denying abortion's risks.

Death From Legal Abortions

A study of pregnancy-associated deaths published in the *American Journal of Obstetrics and Gynecology* demonstrates that the mortality rate associated with legal abortion is 2.95 times higher than that of pregnancies carried to term.[35] A Finland study concluded that "women who abort are approximately four times more likely to die in the following year than women who carry their pregnancies to term."[36]

The Centers for Disease Control reported ten abortion-related deaths in 1998,[37] but according to the same report, such statistics are of limited value because, remarkably, *not all states require reporting*. Abortion clinics have absolutely nothing to gain and much to lose by providing information.[38] What makes abortion-related deaths harder to trace is that the majority of the deaths do not occur during the surgery but afterward, usually after release. Hence, researcher Dr. Brian Clowes states that many secondary reasons are routinely identified as the cause of death:

> Consider the mother who hemorrhaged, was transfused, got hepatitis, and died months later. Official cause of death? Hepatitis. Actual cause? Abortion. A perforated uterus leads to pelvic abscess, sepsis (blood poisoning), and death. The official report of the cause of death may list pelvic abscess and septicemia. Abortion will not be listed. Abortion causes tubal pathology. She has an ectopic pregnancy years later and dies. The cause listed will be ectopic pregnancy. The actual cause? Abortion.[39]

A study published in the *Southern Medical Journal* indicated that "women who have abortions are at significantly higher risk of death than women who give birth."[40] This included a 154 percent higher risk of death from suicide, as well as higher rates of death from accidents and homicides.

Women's Health after Abortion is an encyclopedic work citing more than five hundred medical journal articles, demonstrating the adverse effects of abortion on women.[41] Anyone still doubting that abortion causes serious long-term harm to women should examine this compelling evidence.

Back Alley Abortions?

Fifteen years before abortion became legal in America, around 85 percent of illegal abortions were done by "reputable physicians in good standing in their local medical associations."[42] In 1960 Planned Parenthood stated that "90% of all illegal abortions are presently done by physicians."[43] The vast majority of abortions were not done in back alleys, but in the back offices of licensed physicians.

Were these doctors "butchers," as pro-choice advocates claim? Most of the physicians performing abortions *after* legalization were the same ones doing it *before* legalization. Neither their training nor their equipment improved when abortion was decriminalized. Either they were not butchers before legalization, or they continued to be butchers after legalization. It cannot be argued both ways.

Former abortion-rights activist Bernard Nathanson admits that he and his cofounders of NARAL (National Abortion Rights Action League) fabricated the figure that a million women were getting illegal abortions in America each year. The average, he says, was actually one-tenth that number, about ninety-eight thousand per year. Nonetheless, the media eagerly disseminated the false information. Nathanson says that he and his associates also invented the "nice, round shocking figure" of five thousand to ten thousand deaths a year from illegal abortions.

Years later Nathanson wrote what should have shocked the nation but was largely ignored by the same media that had spread the lies:

> I confess that I knew the figures were totally false, and I suppose the others did too if they stopped to think of it. But in the "morality" of our revolution, it was a useful figure, widely accepted, so why go out of our way to correct it with honest statistics? The overriding concern was to get the laws [against abortion] eliminated, and anything within reason that had to be done was permissible.[44]

Research confirms that in 1966, before the first state legalized abortion, a total of 120 mothers died from abortion.[45] The facts are that the actual number of abortion deaths [of women] in the twenty-five years prior to 1973 averaged 250 a year, with a high of 388 in 1948.[46]

By 1972 abortion was still illegal in 80 percent of the country, but the use of antibiotics had greatly reduced the risk. Hence, the number dropped to thirty-nine maternal deaths from abortion that year.[47] Dr. Christopher Tietze, a prominent statistician associated with Planned Parenthood, maintained that these were accurate figures, with a margin of error no greater than 10 percent.[48]

However, suppose that only one out of five deaths from illegal abortion was properly identified. This would mean that the number of women dying the year before abortion was legalized would be fewer than two hundred, only 2–4 percent of the five thousand to ten thousand per year claimed by pro-choice advocates. This was not mere exaggeration. It was fabrication.

Two Deaths For The Price Of One

Since public health officials stopped looking for abortion-caused deaths after abortion became legal, the opportunity to overlook or cover up abortion-caused deaths became far greater. A former abortion clinic owner told me, "A woman died because of an abortion at our clinic, but the public never heard about it, and it wasn't reported to the authorities as abortion related."[49]

When the *Chicago Sun-Times* investigated Chicago-area abortion clinics in 1978, it uncovered the cases of twelve women who died of legal abortion but whose deaths had not been reported as abortion-related. Twelve unreported deaths from abortion in one small part of the country is a revealing number when the official statistics indicated twenty-one deaths from abortion *in the entire country* the previous year![50]

Legalized abortion has resulted in fourteen times more women having abortions. Writing in the *American Journal of Obstetrics and Gynecology,* Dr. Dennis Cavanaugh stated that since abortion has been legalized, "there has been no major impact on the number of women dying from abortion in the US . . . After all, it really makes no difference whether a woman dies from legal or illegal abortion, she is dead nonetheless."[51]

No Such Thing as a Safe Abortion

Clothes hangers make effective propaganda pieces at pro-choice rallies, but they do not accurately reflect what would happen if abortion were made illegal again. Clothes hangers would be used for baby clothes, but not abortions.

Regarding the frequent reference to "clothes hanger abortions," one woman told me, "People must think women are stupid. If abortion were illegal and I wanted one, I sure wouldn't use a clothes hanger."

Since 90 percent of pre-1973 abortions were done by doctors, it's safe to assume that if abortion were illegal again, many physicians would continue to give abortions. And sadly, yes, many women would continue to have abortions. But the "many" might be a quarter of a million rather than five times that many. There is simply no way to tell. The result might be a million mothers and babies annually saved from abortion.

From the child's point of view, there is no such thing as "a safe, legal abortion." It is always deadly. For every two people who enter an abortion clinic, only one comes out alive.

Rape is a horrible attack on an innocent human being, so we do not attempt to make rape safe and legal. We do not try to make kidnapping or child abuse safe and legal. If abortion does not kill children, let's not oppose it. But if it does kill children, as the evidence clearly indicates, our goal should not be to make it as safe and legal as possible, but to provide alternatives and legal restrictions that help avoid it in the first place. David Reardon states:

> Unfortunately, every horror that was true of illegal abortion is also true about legalized abortion. Many veterans of illegal abortion, however, do not realize this. Instead, they cling to the belief that all the pain and problems they suffered could have been avoided if only abortion had been legal. . . . Instead of recognizing that it is the very nature of abortion itself which caused their problems, they blame their suffering on the illegality of abortion at that time.[52]

Abortion is horrible because it is a process in which instruments of death invade a woman's body and kill her innocent child. Neither laws nor slogans nor attractive waiting rooms nor advanced medical equipment can change that reality.

What Women Say

In surveys of women who experienced post-abortion complications:

1. More than 90 percent said they were not given enough information to make an informed choice.

2. More than 80 percent said it was very unlikely they would have aborted if they had not been so strongly encouraged to abort by others, including their abortion counselors.

3.   Eighty-three percent said they would have carried to term if they had received support from boyfriends, families, or other important people in their lives.[53]

Surely every woman deserves better than what abortion gives her. And surely she deserves not to lose what is taken from her—her own child.

Chapter 12

Is Abortion Right When Pregnancy Presents Risks to the Mother's Life?

Is abortion justified when a woman's life or health is threatened by pregnancy or childbirth? And how often is that actually the case?

While he was US surgeon general, Dr. C. Everett Koop stated that in thirty-six years as a pediatric surgeon, he was never aware of a single situation in which a preborn child's life had to be taken in order to save the mother's life. He said the use of this argument to justify abortion was "a smoke screen."

Dr. Landrum Shettles, pioneer in infertility treatment and called "the father of in vitro fertilization," claimed that less than 1 percent of all abortions were performed to save the mother's life.[1] (With medical science continually improving, surely the likelihood today is no greater than it was nineteen years ago.)

Save The Life That Can Be Saved

A woman with toxemia will have adverse health reactions and considerable inconvenience, including probably needing to lie down for much of her pregnancy. This is difficult, but normally not life-threatening. In such cases, abortion for the sake of "health" would not be lifesaving but life-taking.

At times it is pregnancy itself—because of routine medical appointments and tests—which may serve as a catalyst for discovering an otherwise undetected illness. But serious illnesses that may rarely occur during a pregnancy can still be treated to protect the mother and her baby. Breast cancer is identified in about one out of every three thousand pregnancies and is usually entirely treatable.[2]

Cancer [of any type] during pregnancy is rare, occurring in approximately one out of every 1,000 pregnancies. . . . However, a pregnant woman with cancer is capable of giving birth to a healthy baby, and some cancer treatments are safe during pregnancy. Cancer rarely affects the fetus directly. Although some cancers may spread to the placenta (a temporary organ that connects the mother and fetus), most cancers cannot spread to the fetus itself.[3]

Dr. John Crown, an oncologist who has treated women who are pregnant and discover they have cancer, told his Twitter followers he has never had a case where abortion was necessary to save the mother's life.[4] He writes,

What I say to most patients is, "I know this sounds like the worst thing that could happen but there is a high chance you are going to get two happy outcomes here: you will be cured and the baby will be born normal. That is the most likely outcome. . . ."[5]

Though more prevalent in postmenopausal women,[6] if the mother has a fast-spreading uterine cancer, treatment to save the mother can place the baby's life at risk. Certainly, surgery to remove the cancer may result in the unintended loss of the child's life.

Friends of ours were faced with a situation where removing the mother's life-threatening and rapidly spreading cancer would, unintentionally yet inevitably, result in their unborn child's death. The pregnancy was so early that there wasn't time for the child to develop sufficiently to live outside the womb before both mother and child would die. The surgery was performed to remove the cancer.

But this was in no sense an abortion. The surgery's purpose wasn't to kill the child but to save the mother. The death of the child was a tragic side-effect of lifesaving efforts. This was a consistently pro-life act, since to be pro-life does not mean being pro-life only about babies. It also means being pro-life about women.

Ectopic Pregnancy

Ectopic pregnancies, when gestation takes place outside the uterus, account for an estimated 2 percent[7] of all pregnancies. Most commonly, implantation begins in a fallopian tube but occasionally on an ovary or against the abdominal wall. Usually the pregnancy miscarries without a woman knowing she was pregnant.

According to pro-choice advocates, "Without a doubt, the most frequently presented example of a case in which the mother's life may be in danger if an abortion is not performed is the case of an ectopic pregnancy."[8]

But because of the nature of an ectopic pregnancy, the child would normally have no hope of survival. And surgery may be necessary to save his mother. These are tragic situations, but once again they are not the *intentional* killing of an innocent person who could otherwise survive. In those instances in which both lives are at risk, and when the death of the unborn child occurs in the effort to keep the mother alive, one life saved is clearly better than two lives lost.

Abortion's Role In Ectopic Pregnancies

The US Department of Health and Human Services conducted a twenty-year study on ectopic pregnancy rates which indicated an increase of more than 500 percent since abortion was legalized.[9]

Pro-choice advocates rightly point out that "the most frequently presented example of a case in which the mother's life may be in danger if an abortion is not performed is the case of an ectopic pregnancy."[10]

I object to the term *abortion* in this context, but there is another issue. According to a 2011 report in the *American Journal of Obstetrics and Gynecology*, pregnancies identified as "ectopic" or "tubal" are incorrectly diagnosed an estimated *40 percent of the time.*[11]

Some have assumed that the increase of chemical abortions should substantially decrease the rate of ectopic pregnancy. But a 2009 study concluded there may be "a trend toward increasing ectopic pregnancy rates over a recent 15-year period."[12]

Past studies show that the risk of an ectopic pregnancy is twice as high for women who have had one abortion, and up to four times as high for women with two or more previous abortions.[13]

While abortion is advocated to protect the health of women, studies show consistently that abortion has placed women at greater risk of ectopic pregnancy, by far the greatest pregnancy-related threat to their lives.

Chapter 13

Is Abortion Right When Pregnancy Is Due to Rape or Incest?

S tudies conducted by the pro-choice Guttmacher Institute indicate that two consenting and fertile adults have only a 3–5 percent chance of pregnancy from an act of intercourse. They also indicate there are factors involved in a rape that further reduce these chances for rape victims.[1] The Institute conducted a write-in survey of 1,160 women in 2004 and found 1.5 percent of abortions were reported as due to rape or incest.[2] Another of their studies cited one percent.[3] Other studies have shown that pregnancies due to rape are much rarer, as few as one in a thousand cases.[4]

What's the Real Issue?

Pro-choice advocates divert attention from the vast majority of abortions by focusing on rape because of its well-deserved sympathy factor. Their frequent references to it leave the false impression that pregnancy due to rape is common, rather than rare.

Where does the misconception come from that many pregnancies are due to rape? Fearful young women sometimes attribute their pregnancies to rape to avoid possible condemnation. Norma McCorvey was the young woman called "Roe" in the *Roe v. Wade* case. She elicited sympathy in the court and media because she claimed to be a rape victim, but years later admitted she'd lied and hadn't been raped.[5] (McCorvey has since become an outspoken pro-life advocate and has asked the Supreme Court to review and reverse *Roe v. Wade*.[6])

We have a dear friend who was raped and became pregnant. Because of her circumstances it wasn't best for her to raise the child. She released the baby for adoption into a Christian family. Our friend periodically has contact with the family and her child. It hasn't been easy and her pain has been great—yet her comfort is in knowing her child lives and is loved.

On a television program about abortion, I heard a man say of a child conceived by rape, "Anything of this nature has no rights because it's the product of rape." But how is the nature of this child different from that of any other child?

And why is it that pro-choice advocates are always saying the unborn child is really the *mother's*, not the father's, until she is raped—then suddenly the child is viewed as the *father's*, not the mother's?

The point is not *how* a child was conceived but *that* he was conceived. He is not a despicable "product of rape." He is a unique and wonderful creation of God.

Having and holding an innocent child, whether the mother chooses to keep her or place her for adoption, can do much more good for a victimized woman than the knowledge that an innocent child died in a fruitless attempt to reduce the mother's trauma.

Conceived by Incest

Incest is a horrible crime. Offenders should be punished, and decisive intervention should be taken to remove a girl from the presence of a relative who has sexually abused her. The abuser—*not* the girl or her child—is the offender. Intervention, protection, and ongoing personal help for the girl—not killing an innocent child—is the solution. (Despite popular beliefs, fetal deformity is rare in such cases. If the child has handicaps, however, he still deserves to live.)

Why should Person A be killed because Person B raped or sexually abused Person A's mother? If your father committed a crime, should you go to jail for it? If you found out today that your biological father had raped your mother, and you had been conceived as a result, would you feel you no longer had a right to live?

A woman who heard me speak about this subject told me afterward, sobbing, "My mother was raped as a thirteen-year-old. She gave birth to me, then gave me up for adoption. Every time I've heard people say abortion is okay in cases of rape, I've thought,

'Then I guess I have no right to live.' And if I had been aborted, my children wouldn't be here either."

Let's punish abusers, not the victims. The woman isn't spoiled goods—she's not "goods" at all but a precious human being with value and dignity that even the vilest act cannot take from her. Likewise, the child isn't a cancer to be removed but a living human being to be loved. If the child needs to be placed for an adoption, isn't this a far better solution than taking her life?

And shouldn't we stop telling people who were conceived by rape that they have no right to live?

Abortion Compounds Rape Trauma

Feminists for Life says, "Some women have reported suffering from the trauma of abortion long after the rape trauma has faded."[7] It's hard to imagine a worse therapy for a woman who's been raped than the guilt and turmoil of having her child killed.

In their book *Victims and Victors,* David Reardon and his associates draw on the testimonies of 192 women who experienced pregnancy as the result of rape or incest and 55 children who were conceived through sexual assault. It turns out that when victims of violence speak for themselves, their opinion of abortion is nearly unanimous—and the exact opposite of what most would predict:

> Nearly all the women interviewed in this anecdotal survey said they regretted aborting the babies conceived via rape or incest. Of those giving an opinion, more than 90 percent said they would discourage other victims of sexual violence from having an abortion. On the other hand, among the women profiled in the book who conceived due to rape or incest and carried to term, not one expressed regret about her choice.[8]

Ironically, the violence of rape and the violence of abortion have something in common. Both are done by a more powerful person at the expense of the less powerful.

Abortion doesn't bring healing to a rape victim. Imposing capital punishment on the innocent child of a sex offender does nothing bad to the rapist and nothing good to the woman.

Creating a second victim never undoes the damage to the first.

OTHER IMPORTANT ISSUES

Chapter 14

Do Birth Control Pills Cause Abortion?

What Is a Contraceptive?

Historically, the terms conception and fertilization have been virtually synonymous, both referring to the very beginning of human life. A contraceptive, then, just as it sounds, was something that prevented fertilization (i.e. *contra*dicted *concep*tion). Unfortunately, as touched on earlier, in the last few decades alternative meanings of "conception" and "contraception" have emerged, which have greatly confused the issue.

Eugene F. Diamond wrote an excellent article in *Physician* magazine. Dr. Diamond states:

> Prior to 1976, a "contraceptive" was understood to be an agent that prevented the union of sperm and ovum. In 1976 the American College of Obstetricians and Gynecologists (ACOG), realizing that this definition didn't help its political agenda, arbitrarily changed the definition.
>
> A contraceptive now meant anything that prevented implantation of the blastocyst, which occurs six or seven days after fertilization. Conception, as defined by *Dorland's Illustrated Medical Dictionary* (27th Edition), became "the onset of pregnancy marked by implantation of the blastocyst."
>
> The hidden agenda in ACOG's redefinition of "contraceptive" was to blur the distinction between agents preventing fertilization and those preventing implantation of the week-old embryo. Specifically, abortifacients such as IUDs, combination pills, minipills, progestin-only pills, injectables such as Provera and, more recently, implantables such as Norplant, all are contraceptives by this definition.[1]

The redefinition of "contraceptive" Dr. Diamond speaks of has gradually crept into the medical literature. Because of the change, some medical professionals will state the Pill is only a contraceptive, even if they know it sometimes acts to prevent implantation.

According to the original meaning of *conception*—which is the meaning still held to by the majority of the public and many if not most medical professionals—there is no way any product is acting as a contraceptive when it prevents implantation.

Contraceptives, then, are chemicals or devices that prevent conception or fertilization. A birth control method that sometimes kills an already conceived human being may function as a contraceptive some or most of the time, but some of the time it is *also* an abortifacient.

The problem of "contraceptives" that are really abortifacients is not a new one. Many pro-life Christians, including physicians, have long opposed the use of Intra-Uterine Devices (IUDs), as well as RU-486 ("the abortion pill") and the Emergency Contraceptive Pill (ECP). Some have also opposed Norplant, Depo-Provera, Nu-vaRing, and the "Mini-pill," all of which sometimes or often fail to prevent conception, but succeed in preventing implantation of the six-day-old human being.

"The Pill"

"The Pill" is the popular term for more than forty different commercially available oral contraceptives. In medicine, they are commonly referred to as BCPs (Birth Control Pills), OCs (Oral Contraceptives) and/or OCPs (Oral Contraceptive Pills). They are also called "Combination Pills," because they contain a combination of estrogen and progestin.

More than twelve million American women use the Pill each year. Across the globe it is used by more one hundred million. The question of whether it causes abortions has direct bearing on untold millions of Christians, many of them pro-life, who use and recommend it. After coming to grips with the importance of this issue, and hearing conflicting opinions for many years, I determined to research this question thoroughly and communicate my findings, whether or not I liked what I found. What follows is a summary of my book *Does the Birth Control Pill Cause Abortions?* (Read the complete book online at www.epm.org/bcp.)

According to multiple references throughout the *Physicians' Desk Reference*, which articulate the research findings of all the birth control pill manufacturers, there are *not one* but *three* mechanisms of birth control pills: (1) inhibiting ovulation (the primary mechanism), (2) thickening the cervical mucus, thereby making it more difficult for sperm to travel to the egg, and (3) thinning and shriveling the lining of the uterus to the point that it is unable or less able to facilitate the implantation of the newly fertilized egg. The first two mechanisms are contraceptive. The third is abortive.

When a woman taking the Pill discovers she is pregnant—according to the *Physicians' Desk Reference*'s efficacy rate tables, listed under every contraceptive, this is 3 percent of Pill-takers *each year*—it means that all three of these mechanisms have failed. The third mechanism *sometimes* fails in its role as backup, just as the first and second mechanisms sometimes fail. However, each and every time the third mechanism succeeds, it causes an abortion.

How the Pill Works

As a woman's menstrual cycle progresses, her endometrium gradually gets richer and thicker in preparation for the arrival of any newly conceived child who may be there to attempt implantation. In a natural cycle, unimpeded by the Pill, the endometrium produces an increase in blood vessels, which allow a greater blood supply to bring oxygen and nutrients to the child. There is also an increase in the endometrial stores of glycogen, a sugar that serves as a food source for the blastocyst (child) as soon as he or she implants.

The Pill keeps the woman's body from creating the most hospitable environment for a child, who may die because he lacks the nutrition and oxygen normally offered by a rich endometrium.

Typically, the new person attempts to implant at six days after conception. If implantation is unsuccessful, the child is flushed out of the womb in a miscarriage that may appear to be nothing more than a normal, even if delayed, menstruation. While there are many spontaneous miscarriages, whenever the miscarriage is the result of an environment created by a foreign device or chemical, it is an artificially induced miscarriage—an abortion. This is true even if the mother does not intend it, is not aware of it happening, and would be horrified if she knew.

Ethics Debate

Defenders argue that the Pill may *not* cause abortions, and since it may not, we should feel free to use and prescribe it. Some also say that *if* the Pill causes abortions, these are only "mini-abortions" which occur "prior to or just following implantation."[2] They therefore suggest that there is no ethical dilemma to be resolved. (This would be true, of course, if human life does not begin at conception, but at implantation—a contention for which many of us believe there is no logical, scientific, or biblical evidence.)

In my experience, ironically, it is only pro-lifers who deny the Pill can prevent implantation. This is because only those who oppose abortion are upset by the evidence that the Pill sometimes causes it. Those who accept abortion as legitimate invariably recognize the Pill can prevent implantation. I have had long conversations with experts convincing me of this. When I press the point they have often said "Of course, we know the Pill sometimes serves to prevent implantation of the fertilized egg. What we don't know is how often."

The moral question, then, is this: since we are uncertain about how many abortions it causes, how should we act in light of our uncertainty?

In teaching college ethics courses, I put it this way: If you're driving at night and you think the dark figure ahead on the road *may* be a child, but it *may* just be the shadow of a tree, do you drive into it or do you put on the brakes? What if you think there's a 50 percent chance it's a child? 10 percent chance? 3 percent chance? How certain do you have to be that you may kill a child before you should stop or swerve?

Shouldn't we give the benefit of the doubt to life?

Potentially Fatal Good Intentions

I've frequently been told that because most people's intention in taking the Pill is to prevent conception, not to have an abortion, it's therefore ethical for them to continue taking the Pill.

I certainly agree most women taking the Pill don't intend to get abortions. In fact, I'm convinced 99 percent of them are unaware this is even possible (which is a sad commentary on the lack of informed consent by Pill-takers). But the fact remains that while the *intentions* of those taking the Pill may be harmless, the *results* can be just as fatal.

A nurse giving your child an injection could sincerely intend no harm to your child, but if she unknowingly injects him with a fatal poison, her good intentions will not lessen the tragedy. Whether the nurse has the heart of a murderer or a saint, your child is equally dead. The best intentions do nothing to reverse the most disastrous results.

In this sense, taking the Pill is analogous to playing Russian roulette, but with more chambers and therefore less risk per episode. In Russian roulette, participants usually don't *intend* to shoot themselves. Their intention is irrelevant, however, because if they play the game long enough they just can't beat the odds. Eventually they die.

"Morning-After" or Plan B Pill

In 1997 the FDA approved the use of normal birth control pills as "emergency contraception."[3] It is significant that this "emergency contraception" is merely a combination of several standard birth control pills in higher dosages. An article explains:

> The morning-after pill refers to a regimen of standard birth control pills taken within 72 hours of unprotected sex to prevent an unwanted pregnancy. The pills prevent pregnancy by inhibiting a fertilized egg from implanting itself in the uterus and developing into a fetus.[4]

Of course, the pills do *not* "prevent pregnancy" if we accept the historical understanding that pregnancy begins at conception, not implantation. Acting as if pregnancy begins at implantation takes the emphasis off the baby's objective existence and puts it on the mother's endometrium and its role in sustaining the child that has already been created within her. As *World* magazine points out, "In reality the pill regimen—designed to block a fertilized egg from implanting into the uterus—aborts a pregnancy that's already begun."[5]

The Semantics War

Many speak as if a newly conceived child, with all the chromosomes and DNA in place (depersonalized as a "fertilized egg") is not a living person just because she has not yet settled into her home, the mother's endometrium. Therefore, it is argued, it's fine to make her home hostile to her life. But this is like saying the homeless are not really people since they aren't living in a house. And if homes were built for them, it would be all right to burn down those homes before the people inhabited them, and leave them out in the cold to die.

Whatever prevents implantation kills a unique human being as surely as any later abortion procedure.

How mainstream are "morning-after" (also called Plan B) pills? In February 2012 they were available in vending machines on the campus of Shippensburg University of Pennsylvania. For twenty-five dollars per dose, anyone, including a junior high school girl, can purchase a drug designed to take the life of an already conceived human being.[6]

Why Hide the Truth?

Since preventing implantation isn't of any ethical concern except to those who believe God creates people at the point of conception, it isn't terribly surprising the experts haven't gotten the word out. In their minds, why should they?

Pill manufacturers have their own research departments with dozens of full-time researchers who must produce thousands of pages of findings every year. But these findings are distilled into very small packets of information.

The published indications of Pill-caused abortions is substantial. But it is spread out in dozens of obscure and technical scientific journals. Consequently, not only is the most significant evidence not in print, but relatively few physicians—and almost no one in the general public—have ever seen the most compelling evidence that *is* in print. If they have heard anything at all, it has only been piecemeal.

Many well-meaning physicians, including Christian OB/GYNs and family practitioners, simply are not aware of this evidence. A number of them who have read my book *Can the Birth Control Pill Cause Abortions?* have told me this. And when they read the studies I cite, they are stunned at how compelling the evidence is.

Even when the information about the Pill rises to the surface here and there, so many Christians—including pastors and para-church leaders—have used and recommended the Pill, that we have a natural resistance to raising this issue or looking into it seriously when others raise it.

We also cannot escape the fact that the Pill is a multi-billion dollar worldwide industry. Its manufacturers, the drug companies, have tremendous vested interests. So do many physicians prescribing it. I do *not* mean by this that most physicians prescribe it primarily for financial gain; I do mean it is a significant part of the total income of many practices.

Those best placed to disseminate this information are the Pill manufacturers. The problem, however, is that they gain customers by convincing them the Pill works, *not* by teaching them how it works. No one takes the Pill because she knows it prevents implantation. But some, perhaps many, might stop taking it if they realize it does.

Hence, a pharmaceutical company has nothing to gain, and perhaps a great deal to lose, by drawing attention to this information.

Chapter 15

What about Disabled and Unwanted Children?

Some argue, "It's cruel to let a handicapped child be born to a miserable and meaningless life." But what do the disabled think about their lives? Spina bifida patients were asked whether their handicaps made life meaningless and if they should have been allowed to die after birth. "Their unanimous response was forceful. Of course they wanted to live! In fact, they thought the question was ridiculous."[1]

I heard a pro-choice advocate say of a severely handicapped child, "Should a woman be forced to bring a *monster* into the world?" Only by using such words can we deceive ourselves into believing them. The term *vegetable* is another popular word for disadvantaged humans. Such terminology is cruel and dehumanizing, but doesn't change who they are.

A bruised apple is still an apple. A blind dog is still a dog. A senile woman is still a woman. A handicapped child is still a child. A person's nature and worth aren't changed by a handicap. S. E. Smith, in an article in *Disability* says, "The able-bodied, who control much of society, need to break themselves of the beliefs that life with a disability is tragic, not worth living."[2]

Tests Have Risks and Fail

Some doctors recommend "terminating the pregnancy" (killing the child) if a couple's genetic history suggests a risk of abnormality. Current standard tests for possible deformities are *chorionic villa sampling* (CVS) and *amniocentesis*[3] ("triple test"). Other research focuses on RNA sampling.[4] A 2011 study indicates these tests have associated risks for miscarriage of one in three hundred to one in five hundred.[5] Similarly, the Centers for Disease Control estimate that in early amniocentesis the rate of death to the unborn through miscarriage is "between one in 400 and one in 200 procedures."

This study also found a striking tenfold increase in the risk of clubfoot deformity after early amniocentesis.[6] Ironically, then, a procedure designed to identify fetal deformity actually has a considerable chance of causing it.

"Of all eugenic abortions prescribed on the basis of genetic history one-half to three-quarters of the unborn children destroyed are not affected by the disease. More 'normal' children are killed than 'handicapped' children."[7]

Doctors Aren't Always Right

Many parents have aborted their babies because physicians told them that their children would be severely handicapped. Others I've met were told the same thing, but chose to let their babies live. These parents were then amazed to give birth to normal children.

A few years ago I saw on the television news a woman who was diagnosed as having a growing tumor. The "tumor" turned out to be a child. The woman, who had cancer, had been under extensive chemotherapy for two years. Had her doctors known she was pregnant, she almost certainly would have been advised to get an abortion on the assumption the child would be deformed. Yet the child was perfectly normal.

An Oregon resident went to a Portland medical clinic to have doctors review a CT scan. They interpreted the scan as revealing a large pelvic mass that appeared to be sitting on top of the woman's uterus. The woman underwent surgery for a hysterectomy to remove the presumed tumor. It turned out she did not have cancer, but was sixteen weeks pregnant.

She filed a lawsuit for the loss of her uterus and the loss of her unborn child. Ultimately the Oregon Court of Appeals concluded that her unborn child was not a "person" under Oregon law.

Deformities Are Sometimes Minor

Planned Parenthood's Guttmacher Institute says that 1 percent of women who have abortions have been advised by their doctors that the unborn has a defect.[8] But what are called deformities are sometimes easily correctable conditions, such as cleft lips and cleft palates. After reading in London's *Sunday Times* about these common cosmetic abortions, a mother of a five-year-old girl with a cleft lip and palate wrote to the editor:

> I was horrified to read that many couples now opt for abortion rather than risk having a baby with such a minor physical imperfection. My daughter is not some subnormal freak . . . she can, and does, lead a happy, fulfilled life. . . . What sort of society do we live in when a minor facial deformity, correctable by surgery, is viewed as so abnormal as to merit abortion?[9]

A Cultural Blind Spot

A survey of pediatricians and pediatric surgeons revealed that more than two out of three would go along with parents' wishes to deny lifesaving surgery to a child with Down syndrome.

On the one hand, we provide special parking and elevators for the handicapped. We talk tenderly about those poster children with spina bifida and Down syndrome. We sponsor the Special Olympics and cheer on the competitors, speaking of the joy and inspiration they bring us. But when we hear a woman is carrying one of these very children, many say, "Kill it."

Here in Oregon, in 2012, a couple was awarded nearly three million dollars—the amount they claim the extra care for raising their Down syndrome daughter will cost in what was called a wrongful birth lawsuit. They sued the hospital for negligence after doctors told them prenatal tests showed their child would not have that disability. The hospital's mistake saved the child's life, because the parents claim they would have aborted her had they known.[10] (What message does that send to their child?)

Significantly, with all of the groups that advocate prenatal testing, "there has not been a single organization of parents of mentally retarded children that has ever endorsed abortion."[11]

Suppose your six-year-old becomes blind or paraplegic. He's now a burden. Raising him is expensive, inconvenient, and hard on your mental health. Should you put him to death? If a law were passed that made it legal to put him to death, would you do it? If not, why not?

You wouldn't kill your handicapped child *because you know him*. But killing an unborn child just because you haven't held him in your arms and can't hear his cry doesn't change his value. Give yourself a chance to know your child. You *will* love him.

What about the anencephalic child who doesn't have a fully developed brain? Since the common expectation is "he will die anyway," doctors often advise parents to have an abortion.[12] There are cases that challenge that conclusion,[13] but even if those cases didn't exist, it's one thing to know a child will probably die, and entirely another to choose to take his life.

Choosing Life

A couple attending a Sunday school class I was teaching at my church had discovered that the child she was carrying was anencephalic. Devastated, they requested prayer of the class because "we're meeting with the doctor tomorrow to discuss our options."

Knowing the primary option discussed would be abortion, I waited to see if any of the believers present would offer counsel. A number of sincerely sympathetic people approached them. Yet no one warned them not to follow their physician's counsel if it was to abort. After everyone else had left, I talked with them and they told me they felt hopeless. Based on what the doctor had advised them already, they had decided it would be better to "end it" by an abortion as soon as possible.

I asked them gently, if they were told one of their three older children would die within the next year, would they love that child as long as he lived, or would they "end it" by taking his life? They looked at me with horror. "Of course not!"

They decided to let their baby live. What happened next was not easy, but it became a beautiful experience for their family. The child was born, they named her, and each of their children held her.

They prayed over her and loved her, and took family pictures to-gether. After a few weeks, she died.

They had a memorial service and brought their photos to church, and told me how healing it was for them to go through this together. There was no way to make things easy, but to have taken their child's life would have robbed their family of great richness. The other children will always remember their precious sister, and the parents will always cherish their sweet daughter.

How tragically different it nearly was, and would have been, if they had followed others' advice, including their physician's. (And how often do Christians, even in pro-life churches, fail to step for-ward to help people make the right decisions in light of the sanctity of human life?)

No Justification

Many families have had precious experiences naming, holding, and bonding with an anencephalic baby after birth.[14] This is in stark contrast to the unhealthy grief and guilt that comes from denying a baby's place in the family, and taking his life. Abortion does not eliminate grief.[15] Indeed, it ultimately magnifies it.

In a March 2012 article in the *Journal of Medical Ethics*, two Australian professors, Alberto Giubilini and Francesca Minerva, argued that "after-birth abortion" should "be permissible in all the cases where abortion is, including cases where the newborn is not disabled." The professors cited Down syndrome as an example, noting that "such children might be an unbearable burden on the family and on society as a whole, when the state economically pro-vides for their care." Dr. Jeff Myers responded that such a "barbaric argument is the logical outcome of a pro-abortion stance" and that to say that a child "can be aborted—killed—because circumstances aren't perfect will cast our society back into the eugenics debate that the Nazis exploited so effectively to kill those they deemed undesirable."[16]

The quality of a society is largely defined by how it treats its weakest members. Killing the innocent is never justified because it relieves others of a burden. It's not a solution to inflict suffering on one person in order to avoid it in another. If we abort children because of their handicaps, we jeopardize all handicapped people.

The Burden of Being Unwanted

Planned Parenthood argues that unwanted children "get lower grades, particularly in language skills." It says unwanted adolescents "perform increasingly poorly in school," And "they are less than half as likely as wanted children to pursue higher education."[17]

I don't question the accuracy of these findings. They tell us what we should already know—the importance of wanting our children. Instead, however, pro-choice advocates use such research to justify aborting the "unwanted."

There are "unwanted" pregnancies, but in reality *there is no such thing as an unwanted child*. While certain people may not want them, other people do, desperately.

Nearly 1.3 million American families want to adopt. There's such a demand for babies that private US adoptions can cost up to thirty thousand dollars even without "expensive surprises."[18] Adoptions from outside the United States more than doubled during the 1990s as fewer couples were able to find children to adopt.[19] A black market[20] has developed where babies are stolen[21] and sold for as much as fifty thousand dollars. Not just "normal" babies are wanted; many people request special-needs babies, including those with Down syndrome and spina bifida.[22]

Feelings can change. Many children who are at first unwanted by their mothers are very much wanted later in the pregnancy and even more at birth. (Unfortunately, many women who would have wanted the child by their sixth month of pregnancy get an abortion in their third month.)

Furthermore, many children wanted at birth are *not* wanted when they are crying at 2:00 a.m. six weeks later. Shall whether or not the parents want the baby still determine whether she deserves to live? If that's a legitimate standard before birth, why not after?

The problem of "unwantedness" is a good argument for wanting children. But it's a poor argument for killing them.

One of the most misleading aspects of the pro-choice argument is making it appear that abortion is in the best interests of the baby. This is so absurd as to be laughable were it not so tragic. A little person is torn limb from limb, *for her benefit*? Similarly, slave owners argued that slavery was in the best interest of blacks. (Whom are we kidding?)

People say, "I can't have this child because I can't give it a good life." And what is their solution to not being able to give him a good life? To take from him the only life he has.

Every Child A Wanted Child

Unwanted describes not the child but an attitude of some adults toward the child. The real problem isn't unwanted children, but unwanting adults.

"Wanting" is simply one person's subjective and changeable feeling toward another. The "unwanted" child is a real person regardless of anyone else's feelings toward her.

A woman's worth was once judged by whether or not a man wanted her. A child's worth is now judged by whether or not her mother wants her. Both of these are tragic injustices.

Planned Parenthood's famous slogan, "Every child a wanted child," is something we should all agree with. Where we disagree is in the proper way to finish the sentence. How do *you* think the sentence should be finished?

- *Every child a wanted child,* so . . . let's place children in homes where they are wanted, and let's learn to want children more.

- *Every child a wanted child,* so . . . let's identify unwanted children before they're born and kill them by abortion.

Everyone agrees that children should be wanted. The only question is this: Should we get rid of the *unwanting* or get rid of the *children*?

When it comes to the unborn, the abortion rights position is more accurately reflected in a different slogan, one that doesn't look so good on a bumper sticker: "Every unwanted child a dead child."

Chapter 16

Does Abortion Prevent
Child Abuse?

Ateenage girl delivered a child in a Delaware motel. She and her boyfriend put the baby, still alive, in a plastic bag and dropped it in a Dumpster. A seventeen-year-old mother who was attending night school hurled her baby into the river after she couldn't find a babysitter. Similar stories abound.

In 1973, when abortion was legalized, child abuse cases in the United States were estimated at 167,000 annually.[1] In 2010 there were 701,158 substantiated cases of abuse and 1,262 fatalities, well over four times the rate of abuse before abortion was legalized.[2]

The increase in child abuse is actually far more dramatic than this indicates, since fifty-four million American children killed by surgical abortions (and an unknown number by chemical abortions) *are not counted as victims of child abuse*. Yet abortion is the earliest child abuse, and none other is more deadly.

The pervasive notion that aborting a child prevents child abuse is one of the strangest arguments ever made. It is true in exactly the same sense that this statement is true: *killing one's wife prevents wife abuse*. True, dead people are no longer here to be abused. In that sense, future abuses can be prevented by killing them now. But arguing that we have saved them from abuse by killing them is surely convoluted logic.

But *why* have far more children in America been abused since abortion was legalized than before? I believe a large part of the answer is that *abortion has changed the way we view children*.

Abortion's Link to Child Abuse

Pro-choice advocates argue, "Having more unwanted children results in more child abuse." This has a certain logical appeal, but some significant studies tell a different story.

Decades ago University of Southern California professor Edward Lenoski conducted a landmark study of 674 abused children. He discovered that 91 percent of the parents admitted they had *wanted* the child they abused.[3] The pro-choice argument that it is unwanted children who are destined for abuse may sound logical, but the best study done to date demonstrates it is false.

When abortion advocates argue their case they usually appeal to a single longitudinal study of 120 individuals in what is now the Czech Republic. The study was conducted under the auspices of the American Psychological Association, which holds an official pro-choice policy. The researcher was Henry P. David, an APA associate concerned with global population and family planning policy.[4] Other studies emphatically disagree with David's conclusions.

In 2005 researchers at Bowling Green State University found that mothers who'd had an abortion were 144 percent more likely to abuse their children.[5] "Findings indicated that women who had an abortion history reported more frequent slapping, hitting, kicking or biting, beating, and use of physical punishment compared to women without an abortion history."[6]

Dr. Philip Ney's and Dr. Priscilla Coleman's studies indicate that this is partially due to the guilt and depression caused by abortion, which hinders the mother's ability to bond with future children.[7] Ney documents that having an abortion decreases a parent's natural restraint against feelings of rage toward small children.[8]

Dr. Coleman concluded that the increase in abuse toward born children is accounted for by "unresolved bereavement issues associated with the abortion experience, disruption of mother-child attachment mechanisms, feelings of abortion-related guilt or shame, and/or negative mental health effects of the abortion."[9]

If we think about it, these findings should not surprise us. When they choose abortion, both mother and father override their best natural impulses to care for a helpless child. Having suppressed that preserving instinct, they may be less prone to hold back rage against a newborn's helpless dependence, a toddler's crying, or a preschooler's defiance.[10] If they are unwilling to tolerate the inconvenience of an unborn child, they will be less likely to tolerate the inconveniences of children they do not abort.

Where Abortion Is Legal, No Child Is Safe

The attitude that results in abortion is exactly the same attitude that results in child abuse: children are an inconvenience, and adults have the right not to be inconvenienced. A needy person who constantly interrupts and frustrates me, who encroaches upon my freedoms and interferes with my plans, deserves to be punished (abused) or eliminated (aborted).

Furthermore, if she doesn't abort, the mother can look at her difficult three-year-old and think, "I had the *right* to abort you; I probably should have." The child owes her everything; she owes the child nothing. This causes resentment toward normal parental sacrifice. Even if subconscious, the logic is inescapable: *If it was all right to kill this same child before birth, surely it's all right to slap her around now.*

Of all child homicide cases in the last quarter of the twentieth century, "61 percent were killed by their own parents," 30 percent by mothers.[11]

There's a pervasive notion that children belong to their parents. Adults think they have the same right to dispose of their children after they're born that society assured them they had before the children were born. Once the child-abuse mentality grips a society, it doesn't restrict itself to only one age group. If preborn children aren't safe, no children are safe.

Princeton's Peter Singer says:

> There [is a] lack of any clear boundary between the newborn infant, who is clearly not a person in the ethically relevant sense, and the young child

who is. In our book, *Should the Baby Live?*, my colleague Helga Kuhse and I suggested that a period of twenty-eight days after birth might be allowed before an infant is accepted as having the same right to life as others.[12]

Contemplate this serious proposal from a prestigious Ivy League professor. Children can be tried out by parents, and if parents are not satisfied, they can dispose of them. Children granted a right to life beginning at twenty-eight days after birth? Why not wait until six months? Killing a five-, ten-, or fifteen-year-old child is really just a postnatal abortion, isn't it?

The solution to battering children outside the womb is not battering children inside the womb.

The solution to child abuse isn't doing the abuse *earlier*. It's not doing the abuse at all.

Chapter 17

Can You Be Personally Opposed to Abortion and Be Pro-Choice?

M any people say, "I'm not pro-abortion, but I am pro-choice." But how would you respond to someone who said, "I'm not pro-rape, I'm just pro-choice about rape"? You'd say, "But to be pro-choice about rape *is* to be pro-rape. It is to legitimize rape by passivity or indifference."

In exactly the same way, to be pro-choice about abortion is to be pro-abortion.

At first glance the bumper sticker slogan makes sense: "Against Abortion? Don't Have One." The logic applies perfectly to flying planes, playing football, or eating pizza . . . but not to rape, torture, kidnapping, or murder.

There Is No Middle Ground

Some imagine that being personally opposed to abortion, while believing others have the right to choose it, is some kind of compromise between the pro-abortion and pro-life positions. It isn't.

To the baby who dies, it makes no difference whether those who refused to protect her were *pro-abortion* or "merely" *pro-choice* about abortion.

Being personally against abortion but favoring another's right to abortion is self-contradictory. It's exactly like saying, "I'm personally against child abuse, but I defend my neighbor's right to abuse his child if that is his choice." Or "I'm personally against slave-owning, but if others want to own slaves, that's none of my business." Or, "I'm not personally in favor of wife-beating, but I don't want to impose my morality on others, so I'm pro-choice about wife-beating."

A radio talk show host told me she was offended that some people called her "pro-abortion" instead of "pro-choice." I asked her, on the air, *Why don't you want to be called pro-abortion? Is there something wrong with abortion?*

She responded, "Abortion is tough. It's not like anybody really wants one."

I said, "I don't get it. What makes it tough? Why wouldn't someone want an abortion?"

Frustrated, she said in an impassioned voice, "Well, you know, it's a tough thing to kill your baby!"

The second she said it, she caught herself, but it was too late. In an unguarded moment she'd revealed what she knew, and what everyone knows if they'll only admit it: Abortion is difficult for exactly the same reason it's wrong—*because it's killing a child.*

And there is no justification for child-killing.

The only good reason to oppose abortion is a reason that compels us to say it should not be legal for others. Because it takes away a child's most basic right—*his or her right to live.*

Chapter 18

What about Adoption?

The pro-choice movement, ironically, fosters the idea that women really have *no other choice* but abortion. We might just as well call the pro-choice movement the "no-choice-but-abortion" movement. Many women will testify that for them "pro-choice" really meant just that: "*no* choice."

Father, mother, boyfriend or husband, teachers, school counselors, doctor, nurses, media, and peers often pressure the pregnant woman into making the one choice her conscience tells her is wrong. (But few or none of them will be there to offer support when she realizes what she's done.)

Do women really want abortions? Frederica Mathewes-Green, past president of Feminists for Life, said, "No one wants an abortion as she wants an ice-cream cone or a Porsche. She wants an abortion as an animal, caught in a trap, wants to gnaw off its own leg. Abortion is a tragic attempt to escape a desperate situation by an act of violence and self-loss."[1]

Abortion isn't a free choice as much as a last resort. Most women would choose not to abort if they felt they would get the emotional and financial support they need to complete the pregnancy. A study in Britain suggests that 82 percent of women surveyed stated they "deeply regretted" having had an abortion and were compelled by a lack of information about the long-term effects.[2]

Some women testify that they were coerced, or at least exploited by abortion clinic staff whose job it was to persuade them to get abortions.[3]

Former owners and employees of abortion clinics, including several I have talked with personally, have stated it was their job to "sell abortions" to pregnant women. Some clinics even hire professional marketing experts to train their staff in abortion sales.[4]

A Choice That's Win-Win

The National Council for Adoption reports:

> While there has been a decrease in domestic infant and intercountry adoption over the past several years, there has been no decrease in the number of American families willing to adopt. In fact, the opposite is true; many families wait for years in order to adopt children.[5]

In 2000 the council estimated 1.3 million couples waited to adopt a child.[6] Yet each year, almost the same number of children are being killed by abortion. In 2007 fewer than nineteen thousand new babies were made available for adoption. The number is said to be declining each year.[7]

In a society that values choice, why aren't doctors, schools, family planning clinics, and abortion clinics required to present women with facts about *all* available choices, including adoption? Why aren't they required to say, "If you are willing to wait only four more months, your child can be delivered and placed for adoption in a home where she will be wanted and loved"?

A friend told us, "When I made my living as an abortion clinic counselor, I was totally uninformed of abortion alternatives. I never recommended adoption or keeping the child. I was completely unaware of the medical facts, including the development of the fetus. I received no training in factual matters—my job was just to make sure women went through with their abortions."

With this kind of "counseling," how many women will choose anything other than abortion?

A Guilt-Free Alternative

Adoption is a positive alternative that allows the biological parents not to take on the challenges of child raising, while saving an innocent life *and* making the adoptive family deliriously happy. Yet it is seldom chosen by pregnant women. No wonder, since it is rarely even put before them as an alternative. *Abortion is the default choice*, and often other choices aren't even discussed.

This doesn't mean it is easy for a woman to place her child for adoption. Research with pregnancy care centers indicates emotional resistance to adoption is very common among abortion-bound women.[8] The reason that adoption may be painful is the same reason that abortion is devastating—a human life is involved. Abortion clinic staffs are trained to reinforce a woman's reluctance to giving up her child to others. [9]

Adoption is often portrayed negatively in pro-choice literature. Pro-choice advocates Carole Anderson and Lee Campbell say of adoption, "The unnecessary separation of mothers and children is a cruel, but regrettably usual, punishment that can last a lifetime."[10]

While calling adoption cruel, they fail to mention a woman's lifelong guilt when she realizes she's killed her own child.[11] Adoption is not punishment of a woman who feels she can't raise her child; it's an alternative to killing that child. Tough though it may feel, it's a heaven-sent alternative to one day waking up to the guilt of abortion.

There are many excellent online adoption resources,[12] as well as the comprehensive *Encyclopedia of Adoption,* with more than four hundred informative articles about every aspect of adoption.[13] We owe it to both women and children to be informed about adoption.

Adoption Is Ultimately Good For All Parties

By carrying a child to term, a woman accepts responsibility for her choices. She grows and matures. She can look back with pride and satisfaction that she did the right thing by allowing her child both life and a good family.

Of course, adoption is only one alternative. The woman may choose to raise the baby herself. Either choice can be right. More frequently now, women allow family members to adopt and the baby to stay rooted within the birth mother's family.[14]

One of the most common responses of a pregnant woman considering abortion is, "What kind of mother would I be to give up a child for adoption?" The irony is that a mother who wouldn't give away her child because he's too precious will instead pay a doctor to kill him. We must gently help mothers feeling the weight of their situation to understand that the question to ask isn't "How could I give up my baby for adoption?" but "How could I kill my baby by abortion?"

Even if she's not in a position to care for her child, she can let others love and care for him. That is an act of love on her part, one that will be a source of consolation to her the rest of her life.

Understandably, the woman wants her crisis to end, yet adoption appears for some to leave the situation unresolved "with uncertainty and guilt as far as she can see for both herself and her child."[15] She may feel like she would be not only a mother, but a bad mother, who gave her child away to strangers.

The logic here is based on her wishful thinking that if she aborts, then the child inside her will not be a child and *she will not have been a mother*.

In reality, of course, she cannot choose whether or not to become a mother or whether or not her child is real—both of these are unalterable facts. Her child is real, and therefore she *is* a mother. The only question is, what will she do with her child?

Because she hasn't yet emotionally bonded with her child, abortion may seem an easy solution, while parting with her child after birth, when there has been bonding, would be difficult. But the child's life is just as real before bonding as after.

A Courageous Choice

The woman has three choices: have her child and raise him, have her child and allow another family to raise him, or have her child killed. Though abortion often seems the most expedient solution, ultimately it's the most destructive.

We must help young women to see child raising, adoption, and abortion clearly.

The pregnant teenager we took into our home previously had two abortions, but while with us gave birth and released her baby for adoption. It wasn't easy, but this wonderful woman, years later, told me: "I look back at the three babies I no longer have, but with very different feelings. The two I aborted fill me with grief and regret.

But when I think of the one I gave up for adoption, I'm filled with joy, because I know he's being raised by a family that wanted him."

The Christian community should make a concerted effort to overcome the negative spin on adoption. We should speak of it positively and show high regard for women who release their children for adoption. We should publicly honor adoptive parents and bless adopted children. We should make prominent the excellent resources on adoption and celebrate it in our churches. We should portray adoption for what it is: a courageous choice that will give life to a child and incredible joy to a family. Only by doing so can we help women realize adoption is a choice for which both they and their child will later be profoundly thankful.

SPIRITUAL PERSPECTIVES AND OPPORTUNITIES

Chapter 19

Will God Forgive Abortions?

illions of women and men, both in society as a whole and in our churches, are suffering under the guilt of abortion.

The heavy emotional burden of abortion isn't limited to those who've had one. A schoolteacher in her forties said, "Advising my daughter to have an abortion led me into a long, suicidal siege. I'm not over it yet."[1]

If you're a woman who's had an abortion, or if you're a man or woman who has advised another—perhaps friend, wife, or daughter—to have one, or have aided them in doing so, this chapter is for you.

It's counterproductive to try to eliminate guilt feelings without dealing with guilt's cause. Others may say, "You have nothing to feel guilty about," but you know better. Only by denying reality can you avoid guilt feelings. And you are tired of pretending.

After all, denial sets you up for emotional collapse whenever something reminds you of the child you once carried. You need a permanent solution to your guilt problem, a solution based on reality, not pretense.

Because the Bible offers that solution, I will quote from it. You may wish to ask your church leader, women's group leader, or a Christian friend or family member to help you understand what follows.

Good News, Bad News

The good news is that God loves you and desires to forgive you for your abortion—and for any and every other sin—whether or not you knew what you were doing. But before the good news can be appreciated, we must know the bad news. The bad news is: true moral guilt exists—all of us are guilty of many moral offenses against God; abortion is only one. "All have sinned and fall short of the glory of God" (Rom. 3:23).

Sin is failing to live up to God's holy standards. It separates us from a relationship with God (Isa. 59:2). Sin deceives us, making us think that *wrong is right* and *right is wrong* (Prov. 14:12). "The wages of sin is death, but the gift of God is eternal life in Christ Jesus our Lord" (Rom. 6:23).

Jesus Christ, God's Son, loved us so much that He became a member of the human race to deliver us from our sin problem (John 3:16). He identified with us in our weakness without being tainted by our sin (Heb. 2:17–18; 4:15–16). Jesus died on the cross as the only One worthy to pay the penalty for our sins demanded by God's holiness (2 Cor. 5:21). He rose from the grave, defeating sin and conquering death (1 Cor. 15:3–4, 54–57).

When Christ died on the cross, shedding His blood for our sins, He said, "It is finished" (John 19:30). The Greek word translated "it is finished" was written across certificates of debt when they were canceled. It meant "paid in full." Christ died to fully pay our debt.

Full Forgiveness

Because of Christ's work on the cross on our behalf, God freely offers us forgiveness. Here are just a few of those offers:

> He does not treat us as our sins deserve
> or repay us according to our iniquities. . . .
> As far as the east is from the west,
> so far has he removed our transgressions from us.
>
> As a father has compassion on his children,
> so the LORD has compassion on those who fear him.
> (Ps. 103:10, 12–13)

> If we confess our sins, he is faithful and just and will forgive us our sins and purify us from all unrighteousness. (1 John 1:9)

> Therefore, there is now no condemnation for those who are in Christ Jesus. (Rom. 8:1)

A Gift That Can't Be Earned

Salvation is a gift dependent not on our merit or efforts, but solely on Christ's sacrifice—"For it is by grace you have been saved, through faith—and this not from yourselves, it is the gift of God—not by works, so that no one can boast" (Eph. 2:8–9). This gift cannot be worked for, earned, or achieved.

God offers us the gift of forgiveness and eternal life, but it's not automatically ours. In order to have the gift we must choose to accept it. We must place our faith in Jesus Christ alone to be our Savior and deliver us from guilt and punishment.

You may think, "But I don't deserve forgiveness after all I've done." That's exactly right. None of us deserves forgiveness. If we deserved it, we wouldn't need it. That's the point of grace. Christ got what we deserved on the cross, so we could get what we don't deserve—a clean slate, a fresh start. None of us are good enough to save ourselves or bad enough to be unforgivable.

Once forgiven, we can look forward to spending eternity with Christ and our spiritual family (John 14:1–3; Rev. 20:11–22:6). You can look forward to being reunited in heaven with your loved ones who are also covered by Christ's sacrifice (1 Thess. 4:13–18).

No Need To Dwell On Past Sins

A promiscuous woman wept at Christ's feet, kissed them, and wiped them with her hair. Jesus said to a judgmental bystander, "Therefore, I tell you, her many sins have been forgiven—for she loved much" (Luke 7:47). Jesus offers the same forgiveness to all of us.

God doesn't want you to go through life punishing yourself for your abortion or for any other wrong you've done. Your part is to accept Christ's atonement, not to repeat it. Jesus said to an immoral woman, "Your sins are forgiven. . . . Your faith has saved you; go in peace" (Luke 7:48, 50). Women rejected by society came to Jesus, and He welcomed them with compassion and forgiveness.

No matter what you've done, no sin is beyond the reach of God's grace. He has seen us at our worst and still loves us. There are no limits to His forgiving grace. And there is no freedom like the freedom of forgiveness.

You may feel immediately cleansed when you confess your sins, or you may need help working through it. Either way, you're forgiven. You should work to forget what lies behind and move on to a positive future made possible by Christ (Phil. 3:13–14). Whenever we start feeling unforgiven, it's time to go back to the Bible and remind ourselves and each other of God's forgiveness.

Joining a group for post-abortion healing can help you immensely. There are post-abortion Bible studies designed for women, and others for men. Many online resources can help you find the support group you need.[2]

Forgiveness Followed By Right Choices

Many women who've had abortions carry understandable bitterness toward the men who used and abused them, toward parents who pressured them, and toward those who misled them into a choice that resulted in their child's death. God expects us to take the forgiveness He's given us and extend it to others (Matt. 6:14–15).

You need to become part of a therapeutic community, a family of Christians called a church. (If you're already in a church, share your abortion experience with someone to get the specific help you need.) You may feel self-conscious around Christians because of your past. You shouldn't. A true Christ-centered church isn't a showcase for saints but a hospital for sinners. The people you're joining are just as human and just as imperfect as you. Most church people understand forgiveness, and are not self-righteous. Those who are should be pitied because they don't comprehend God's grace.

A good church will teach the truths of the Bible and will provide love, acceptance, and support for you. If you cannot find such a church in your area, contact our organization (listed in the back of this book) and we'll gladly help you, as we've helped many others.

A healthy step you can take is to reach out to women experiencing unwelcome pregnancies. God can eventually use your experience to equip you to help others and to share with them God's love.

My wife and I have a number of good friends who've had abortions. Through their caring pro-life efforts they've given to other women the help they wish someone had given them. Telling their stories has not only saved children's lives, and saved mothers from the pain of abortion, but has helped bring healing to them. It can do the same for you.

Chapter 20

Pro-Life Issues: Distraction from the Great Commission or Part of It?

Many well-meaning Christians believe that churches shouldn't mention abortion. Some say that by talking about abortion we'll make people feel guilty. But the reason for talking about it is to *prevent* abortion and the guilt it brings, and to offer help and hope to those who are guilt-ridden and need to be free. That our churches are filled with people who've been involved with abortion is a poor reason for keeping silent about it. In fact, it's the best argument for offering all the perspective, help, and support we can.

A seminary student at my church told me something I've often heard: "Issues like abortion are just a distraction from the main thing."

"What's the main thing?" I asked.

"The great commission," he said. "Winning people to Christ. Everything else is a distraction."

He was referring to Christ's words in Matthew 28:19–20: "Therefore go and make disciples of all nations, baptizing them in the name of the Father and of the Son and of the Holy Spirit, and teaching them to obey everything I have commanded you."

Was he right? Is pro-life action a distraction from the great commission . . . or is it part of it?

As his pastoral advisor, I asked this seminary student about sharing his faith with others. He explained that since he'd come to seminary, he hadn't spent any time with non-Christians.

I said, "Well, pro-life work couldn't distract you from the 'main thing,' since you're not doing the main thing." I then gave him many examples of people who have come to Christ through outreach in the pro-life arena, including the pregnant teenager who lived with us.

Shop, or Save Babies?

One Saturday I was with a group at an abortion clinic. Two Bible college students stopped by and one said, with a disapproving tone, "Why are you here? Why aren't you doing door-to-door evangelism?"

I asked, "Is that what you're doing today?"

No, they had to admit. They were shopping.

So if it's okay to be shopping, studying, or home doing yard work or watching a ball game, why wouldn't it be okay to stand at an abortion clinic offering an opportunity for people to reconsider their decision to kill their child?

I was able to tell the students that only an hour earlier we had shared the gospel with a woman at the clinic who then placed her trust in Christ.

My point was that if the great commission were only about sharing the gospel, pro-life work would still qualify because it presents many opportunities to do just that. But, in fact, there is actually more to the great commission than sharing the gospel.

A Man Named William

Two hundred years ago there lived an Englishman named William, an outspoken slavery opponent who boycotted sugar from the West Indies because it was the product of slavery. William sensed God wanted him to go to India where he was shocked to discover that many Hindus exposed their infant children to die. They also abandoned the weak, sick, and lepers. The British government in India looked the other way because it didn't want to interfere with the culture or religion, but William felt compelled to interfere because people were dying.

One day William witnessed the practice called *sati*, where widows were burned alive on the funeral pyre of their deceased husbands. After seeing one such death, he stood up in front of a group assembled to burn a woman alive and told them the practice was wrong. He led a group of missionaries in protest. He set up public debates on the subject to bring God's perspective to light.

On Sunday morning, December 6, 1829, after years of activism, William received the official decree forbidding widow burning. He was scheduled to preach in church that morning but he didn't. Instead, he dedicated the whole day to translating the decree into the Bengali language because he knew that lives hung in the balance.

Some criticized William for his moral and political actions. They said, "That's not what you're here for. Focus on the main thing. Just preach the gospel and pray."

Who was this social activist so concerned about morality and laws and saving human lives? His name was William Carey, known today as the "Father of Modern Missions." When we think of the great commission and the modern missions movement, no other name is as prominent as his.

Carey went to India to win people to Christ and disciple them, not just by sharing the gospel, but by living it—which included intervening to save lives and laboring to change public opinion and evil laws.

Footsteps To Follow

Some Christians make the mistake of thinking social activism or politics are the answer to everything. They certainly are not. But most modern evangelical churches have lost their activist heritage.

For instance, in 1835 there was a meeting of the New England Anti-Slavery Society. Two thirds of the delegates were ministers.

In the pre-Civil War era Christians were the backbone of the Underground Railroad that illegally housed, fed, and transported slaves escaping to freedom.

The practice of dueling in America was finally outlawed because so many ministers condemned it from their pulpits. They urged their congregations not to vote for any candidate who believed in dueling.

When New York City was dominated by corrupt strong-arm politics of Tammany Hall early in the twentieth century, it was a minister, Charles Parkhurst, who stood against it when no one else would. He was told to just preach the gospel and get out of politics. But he produced 284 affidavits against corruption, which he read from his pulpit, prompting the judicial action that finally curtailed it.

Churches: Once The Nation's Conscience

The moral decline of our nation is partly due to Christians withdrawing from their God-given role, choosing to stay away from controversy, and look the other way while innocent blood is shed.

John Wesley actively opposed slavery. Charles Finney had a major role in the illegal Underground Railroad. D. L. Moody opened homes for underprivileged girls, rescuing them from exploitation. Charles Spurgeon built homes to help care for elderly women and to rescue orphans from the streets of London. Amy Carmichael intervened for sexually exploited girls in India, rescuing them from temple prostitution. She built them homes, a school, and a hospital.

All of these Christians are known as missionaries and evangelists, people who carried out the great commission. Yet we rarely pay attention to their radical commitment to personal and social intervention for the weak, needy, and exploited.

Perhaps their evangelism was effective because they lived out the gospel that they preached. There is no conflict between the gospel and social concern and personal intervention for the needy. In fact there is a direct connection between them.

Part Of The "Main Thing"

We should try to save lives for the simple reason that the Bible our churches preach from every week says we should:

Rescue those being led away to death. (Prov. 24:11)

Defend the cause of the weak and fatherless; maintain the rights of the poor and oppressed. (Ps. 82:3)

Love your neighbor as yourself. (Matt. 19:19)

God's people are to give special care to women without husbands and children without fathers (James 1:27). Who qualifies more for this care than an unmarried woman and her unborn child?

Nothing opens doors for evangelism like need-meeting ministries. Students who do a speech on abortion have follow-up conversations that can lead to sharing the gospel. Those who work at pregnancy centers have great opportunities to share Christ, as do those who pass out literature at abortion clinics and go on campuses to educate about abortion. People who open their homes to pregnant women demonstrate a love which leads to sharing the gospel. Whenever we meet people's needs, evangelism becomes both natural and credible.

Three Perspectives On The Great Commission

We need to consider three things to understand the relationship between pro-life efforts and the great commission.

First, Jesus called loving God "the first and greatest commandment," and loving your neighbor the second greatest, flowing from the first (Matt. 22:37–39).

Obeying the great commission is only one of the ways we are to fulfill the greatest commandments to love God, and to love our neighbors. We also demonstrate love for God and love for children by obeying His commands to oppose the shedding of innocent blood, and to "speak up for those who cannot speak for themselves. . . . defend the rights of the poor and needy" (Prov. 31:8–9).

We are never called to turn our backs on the great *commandment* to fulfill the great *commission*.

Second, even if evangelism were all there was to the great commission, standing up for those whose lives are endangered would qualify because it provides significant opportunities for evangelism. I spoke at a single pregnancy center where in the previous twelve years counselors had led more than two thousand people to faith in Christ, many of whom had become part of local churches in that community.

Third, in His great commission Jesus didn't tell His apostles only to evangelize. He told them (and through them, us) to be "teaching them to obey *everything* I have commanded you" (Matt. 28:20, italics mine). He didn't just say teaching them to *believe;* He said teaching them to *obey.*

Read Matthew 25:31–46, Christ's words about the sheep and goats. Our Lord makes a distinction of eternal significance based not merely on what people believe and preach, but on what they actually do for the weak and needy.

Can anyone read this passage and still believe that intervening for the needy, including unborn children, is some peripheral issue that distracts the church from its main business? On the contrary, doesn't Jesus suggest it is a central part of its main business? It's part of "everything I have commanded you."

So, if we fail to obey Christ's command to care for the needy in His name, and if we fail to teach others to obey it, then we are *not* fulfilling the great commission.

If the church speaks the gospel message far and wide, but doesn't intervene for unborn children and their mothers, and if we don't teach our people to help them, then we are not fulfilling the entire great commission, only one part of it.

Churches are to be the backbone of God's work for the needy. If your church isn't doing enough for the unborn and their mothers, then perhaps God is calling you to step forward and help your church and its leaders take on this vital ministry.

Lessons From The Good Samaritan

Finally, in Luke 10:25–37, to a man who wished to define "neighbor" in a way that excluded certain groups of needy people, Christ told the story of the Good Samaritan, and said, "Go and do likewise."

A busy traveler went out of his way to give physical help to the man lying in the ditch. In contrast, a priest and Levite, respected religious leaders, looked the other way because they had more important "spiritual" things to do.

We Bible-believing Christians are the priests and Levites of our day. Are we paying attention to people lying in ditches, hungry people, victims of sexual trafficking, and abused and aborted children?

Was it a *distraction* from the main thing to help save the life of the man lying in the ditch? Or was it *part* of the main thing? To the priest and Levite it was a distraction. They had sermons to preach, tithes to collect, synagogues to build. But Christ condemned them for failing to help the weak and vulnerable and needy, and He commended the Samaritan for getting down in the ditch where the problem was and giving a dying man his help.

If you were the man whose life was saved, and you heard someone talk about God, who would you listen to, the spiritual sounding, theologically correct priest and Levite who ignored you, or the Samaritan who actually helped you?

What we really need is Christians who, like Jesus, are full of grace and truth. People with both sound doctrine and warm hearts, reaching out to all the needy—not just the unborn and their mothers but including them—in the name of Christ.

Chapter 21

How Can I Help Unborn Babies and Their Mothers?

There are many excellent pro-life organizations across the country and around the world. They specialize in a wide variety of activities that include abstinence education, fetal development education, counseling pregnant women, influencing legislation, offering adoptions, confronting our culture about the prenatal holocaust, picketing abortion clinics, disseminating scientific and psychological studies, prayer, sidewalk counseling outside abortion clinics, and helping post-abortive women and men. There are trained consultants offering counseling and answering toll-free phone calls and e-mail twenty-four hours a day.[1]

A Plea For Pro-Life Unity

This is the fourth decade in which I've had the privilege of working with and observing a wide variety of pro-life ministries. I've seen the great strengths in different approaches, which reach different audiences and attract different volunteers and supporters.

Pro-lifers, understandably passionate about their cause, sometimes assume that their particular form of pro-life ministry is the most important way, the right way, or even the *only* way. This is as shortsighted as it would be for a sailor to say Army Rangers aren't doing important work and they should all be Navy SEALs instead. The pro-life task is huge and multifaceted, calling for multiple strategies. We should *not* all be trying to do the same thing.

We're commanded, "All of you, live in harmony with one another; be sympathetic, love as brothers, be compassionate and humble" (1 Pet. 3:8). Humble minds and tender hearts are quick to learn from others with different personalities, gifts, passions, and strategies. We need gentleness, patience, love, peace, and unity in God's Spirit (Eph. 4:1–6).

For years I led a bimonthly meeting of pro-life leaders from a wide spectrum of groups. We got to know, understand, and learn from each other. We found activities we could cooperate in and discovered we'd been trying to reinvent the wheel in creating materials and programs other groups already had in place. Many commented to me that they'd never understood some of the other groups and had been suspicious of their approach. They'd even felt competitive. But as they got to know these people, they saw their hearts and understood their goals. They came to love and appreciate the brothers and sisters God had called to different aspects of pro-life ministry.

Look for the best organizations to fit your background, personality, gifting, and sense of God's calling. Contact information is available for a wide variety of fine pro-life organizations—national, regional and local.[2] If you need help finding a pro-life group in your area, contact our office for assistance.[3]

What You Can Do

If you're part of a Christ-centered, Bible-teaching church, ask your leaders about pro-life ministry in your church and community. (If you're not part of such a church, find one.) We must resist the notion that "I'm just one person, we're just one small church; we can't make a difference." You can't eliminate need, but you can be used of God to meet needs in exciting ways. How do you help millions of needy people? One person at a time.

The following are not things everyone should do, but merely a menu from which to choose what best suits your gifts and your resources:

1. *Open your home.* Help a pregnant girl needing a place to live, or welcome an "unwanted" child for foster care or adoption. Or devote one day a week to watching the children of single mothers.

2. *Volunteer your time, talents, and services.* Give personal care to pregnant women, newborns, drug babies, orphans, the handicapped, the elderly, street people, and others in need.

Donate time, equipment, furniture, clothes, professional skills, and money to pregnancy centers, adoption ministries, women's homes, abstinence agencies, and right-to-life educational and political organizations and other pro-life groups. Mow their lawn, do their cleaning or plumbing. Design their website, fix their computers.

3. **Be an initiator or activist.** If there's not a pro-life ministry nearby, consider starting one. Build a coalition. Consider renting space next to an abortion clinic or Planned Parenthood office. Establish a pregnancy counseling clinic or pro-life information center. Recruit volunteers. Develop a beautiful memorial to the unborn, perhaps in the form of a rose garden, on your church property or in your community.[4]

4. **Become thoroughly informed.** Know the facts so you can rehearse in advance the best responses to pro-choice arguments.[5] Attend one of the excellent Justice for All training seminars and outreach events.[6] There are many outstanding pro-life websites[7] as well as books, audios, videos, and (usually free) pro-life newsletters.

While surgical abortions have decreased some, chemical abortions are increasing. Learn about chemicals, including RU-486, the abortion pill, also called "the morning-after pill." Investigate NuvaRing, Implanon, Norplant (no longer available in the United States), Depo-Provera, and the Pill. Acquaint yourself with the processes of pregnancy and how these products can each act to interfere with or prevent the newly conceived person from implanting in the endometrium.[8] Choose to care about unborn babies at all stages of their life and development. Become educated about procedures used to kill them, whether surgically or through abortifacient drugs. Become informed enough to draw your own conclusions.

5. **Talk to your friends, neighbors, and coworkers.** Graciously challenge others to rethink their assumptions. Give them a copy

of this book, with some pages marked for their attention. Study the issues in more detail in my larger book *ProLife Answers to ProChoice Arguments*. Give away novels with a pro-life theme, such as *The Atonement Child* by Francine Rivers, *Tears in a Bottle* by Sylvia Bambola, and my book *Deadline*. Direct them to an excellent pro-life educational website: www.Abort73.com.

6. ***Promote discussions of abortion.*** Share pro-life perspectives on social media sites. (We do this regularly through Facebook and Twitter, and you are welcome to reuse anything we post.[9]) Consider establishing your own pro-life website.

   Call in and speak up on talk shows. Ask for equal time on television and radio stations that present the pro-choice position. Order and distribute pro-life literature. Speak up so pro-choice propaganda doesn't go unchallenged.

   As I state in my book *The Grace and Truth Paradox*, it's vitally important that we approach subjects such as abortion in a Christlike manner. Jesus came full of grace and truth (John 1:14). If people are to see Jesus in us, we must offer the truth with grace.

7. ***Write letters.*** Be courteous, concise, accurate, and memorable. Quote brief references cited in this book and my larger book *ProLife Answers to ProChoice Arguments*. Your letter to the editor in a national magazine or major newspaper may be read by hundreds of thousands.

8. ***Encourage business boycotts of abortion clinics.*** Contact influential people including landlords, businesses, insurance providers, medical providers, and various service providers, graciously stating that you cannot in good conscience patronize those who lend their services to the killing of children. If you own a business and are asked to bid on work for an abortion clinic, respectfully explain why no amount of money could compel you to help that enterprise.

9. **Be active in the political process.** Meet with your representatives and share your views on abortion. Draft, circulate, and sign petitions for pro-life ballot measures. Run for political office, school board, or precinct chairman. Stand by pro-life candidates with your time and money. Vote.

10. **Organize or join a pro-life task force in your church.** Respectfully ask to speak with your pastors or leaders. Tell them you feel God prompting you to stand up for unborn children. Do not expect them to do everything, but tell them that you want to serve them and the church, and you will gladly work hard behind the scenes and you don't need to get credit. Give them literature and ask them to watch a video.[10] Give them a statement about abortion I wrote for our church, for Sanctity of Human Life Sunday, and tell them they are welcome to use it (www.epm.org/unbornhandout).

    Recruit positive people who are supportive of the church's other ministries to help you formulate and implement a plan of education and mobilization. Request periodic special offerings for pro-life ministries. Create or order bulletin inserts and literature for your church to distribute.[11] Contact Eternal Perspective Ministries for a wide range of pro-life handouts and web resources.

11. **Acquire Why Pro-Life? at quantity rates and distribute a copy to every family in your church.** (Available at www.epm.org. All royalties from this book go to pro-life ministries; none go to the author.) If your church leaders want ideas for preparing their messages, offer to provide them with some of the many fine resources that have been made available to you.[12]

12. **Use some of the many excellent pro-life resources.** Show in church services or classes pro-life videos such as the powerful *180* DVD (www.180movie.com) and others on abortion or prenatal life.[13] Prayerfully consider showing your church or small group a video that depicts abortions.[14] (Prepare people

and warn them in advance it's not for children.) Distribute contact information for a variety of pro-life groups in your community. Place a bench ad or a billboard with an 800 number for pregnant women to call. Start a group for sidewalk counselors; plan a prayer vigil or a protest. Contact the pro-life groups in your area. They know a lot you don't, and they'll be glad to serve as a resource.

13. *Use the outstanding pro-life curriculum "Abortion Is about God"* developed by Bethlehem Baptist Church. See http://www.bcspress.org/abortion.

14. *Pray daily for pro-life ministries, churches, church leaders, mothers, and babies.* Organize a prayer group. If the darkness of child-killing is to be overcome with the light of truth and compassion, it will require spiritual warfare fought with humble and persistent prayer (Eph. 6:10–20).

15. *Give to pro-life organizations.* I've seen close-up a wide variety of pro-life ministries. In nearly every case I've walked away impressed with the difference that's being made. I encourage you and your church to find a few pro-life organizations in your area, or one of the national or international pro-life ministries, and give generously to them.

Ask yourself, Five minutes after I die, what will I wish I would have done for and given on behalf of the helpless while I still had the chance? Why not spend the rest of our lives closing the gap between what we'll wish we would have given and what we are giving?

We have a brief opportunity—a lifetime on earth—to use our resources to make a difference for eternity. Picture the moment in heaven, and think how you'll feel when someone approaches you, smiling broadly, and says, "Thank you! Your gifts helped save my life . . . and my child's" (or, "my mother's").

Appendices

Abortion in the Bible and Church History

There is a small but influential circle of pro-choice advocates who claim to base their beliefs on the Bible. They maintain that "nowhere does the Bible prohibit abortion."[1] Yet the Bible clearly prohibits the killing of innocent people (Exod. 20:13). All that is necessary to prove a biblical prohibition of abortion is to demonstrate that the Bible considers the unborn to be human beings.

Personhood in the Bible

A number of ancient societies opposed abortion,[2] but ancient Hebrew society had the clearest reasons for doing so because of its foundations in Scriptures. The Bible gives theological certainty to the biological evidence. It teaches that men and women are made in the image of God (Gen. 1:27). As the climax of God's creation, mankind has an intrinsic worth far greater than that of the animal kingdom placed under His care. Throughout the Scriptures, personhood is never measured by age, stage of development, or mental, physical, or social skills. Personhood is endowed by God at the moment of creation—before which there was not a human being and after which there is. That moment of creation can be nothing other than the moment of conception.

The Hebrew word used in the Old Testament to refer to the unborn (Exod. 21:22–25) is *yeled*, a word that "generally indicates young children, but may refer to teens or even young adults."[3] The Hebrews did not have or need a separate word for unborn children. They were just like any other children, only younger. In the Bible there are references to born children and unborn children, but there is no such thing as potential, incipient, or "almost" children.

Job graphically described the way God created him before he was born (Job 10:8–12). The person in the womb was not something that might become Job, but someone who was Job, just younger and smaller. God identifies Himself to Isaiah as, "he who made you, who formed you in the womb" (Isa. 44:2). What each person is, not merely what he might become, was present in his mother's womb.

Psalm 139:13–16 paints a graphic picture of the intimate involvement of God with a preborn person. God created David's "inmost being," not at birth, but before birth. David says to his Creator, "You knit me together in my mother's womb." Each person, regardless of his parentage or handicap, has not been manufactured on a cosmic assembly line, but has been personally knitted together by God. All the days of his life have been planned out by God before any have come to be (Ps. 139:16).

As a member of the human race that has rejected God, each person sinned "in Adam," and is therefore a sinner from his very beginning (Rom. 5:12–19). David says, "Surely I was sinful at birth." Then he goes back even before birth to the actual beginning of his life, saying he was "sinful from the time my mother conceived me" (Ps. 51:5). Each person has a sinful nature from the point of conception. Who but an actual person can have a moral nature? Rocks and trees and animals and human organs do not have moral natures, good or bad.

Jacob was given prominence over his twin Esau "before the twins were born" (Rom. 9:11). When Rebekah was pregnant with Jacob and Esau, Scripture says, "The babies jostled each other within her" (Gen. 25:22). The unborn are regarded as "babies" in the full sense of the term. God tells Jeremiah, "Before I formed you in the womb I knew you" (Jer. 1:5). He could not know Jeremiah in his mother's womb unless Jeremiah, the person, was present there. The Creator is involved in an intimate knowing relationship not only with born people, but with unborn people.

In Luke 1:41 and 44 there are references to the unborn John the Baptist, who was at the end of his second trimester in the womb. The Greek word translated as "baby" in these verses is the word *brephos*.

It is the same word used for the already born baby Jesus (Luke 2:12, 16) and for the babies brought to Jesus to receive His blessing (Luke 18:15–17). It is also the same word used in Acts 7:19 for the newborn babies killed by Pharaoh. To the writers of the New Testament, like the Old, a baby is simply a baby, whether born or unborn.

The angel Gabriel told Mary that she would be "with child and give birth to a son" (Luke 1:31). In the first century, and in every century, to be pregnant is to be with child, not with that which might become a child. The Scriptures teach the unity of the whole person, body, soul, and spirit (1 Thess. 5:23). Wherever there is a living genetically distinct human being, there is a living soul and spirit.

The Status of the Unborn

One scholar states: "Looking at Old Testament law from a proper cultural and historical context, it is evident that the life of the unborn is put on the same par as a person outside the womb."[4] When understood as a reference to miscarriage Exodus 21:22–25 is sometimes used as evidence that the unborn is subhuman. But a proper understanding of the passage shows the reference is not to a miscarriage, but to a premature birth, and that the "injury" referred to, which is to be compensated for like all other injuries, applies to the child as well as to his mother. This means that, "far from justifying permissive abortion, it in fact grants the unborn child a status in the eyes of the law equal to the mother's."[5]

Meredith Kline observes, "The most significant thing about abortion legislation in Biblical law is that there is none. It was so unthinkable that an Israelite woman should desire an abortion that there was no need to mention this offense in the criminal code."[6] All that was necessary to prohibit an abortion was the command, "You shall not murder" (Exod. 20:13). Every Israelite knew that the preborn child was indeed a child. Therefore, miscarriage was viewed as the loss of a child and abortion as the killing of a child.

Numbers 5:11–31 is an unusual passage of Scripture used to make a central argument in *A Pro-choice Bible Study*, published by Episcopalians for Religious Freedom.[7] They cite the New English Bible's peculiar translation which makes it sound as if God brings a miscarriage on a woman if she is unfaithful to her husband. Other translations refer to a wasting of the thigh and a swelling of her abdomen, but do not take it to mean pregnancy, which would presumably be called what it is.

It appears that God was expected to do some kind of miracle related to the bitter water, creating a dramatic physical reaction if adultery had been committed. The text gives no indication of either pregnancy or abortion. Indeed, in the majority of cases of suspected adultery, there would be no pregnancy and therefore no child at risk.

The *Pro-choice Bible Study* that cites the NEB's unique translation suggests if God indeed causes a miscarriage, it would therefore be an endorsement of people causing abortions. This is a huge stretch, since neither the wife, husband, nor priest made the decision to induce an abortion, nor would they have had the right to do so. The passage does not seem to refer to a miscarriage at all; but even if it did, there is certainly nothing to suggest any endorsement of human beings initiating an abortion.

Child Sacrifice

Child sacrifice is condemned throughout Scripture. Only the most degraded societies tolerated such evil, and the worst of these celebrated it as if it were a virtue. Ancient dumping grounds have been found filled with the bones of hundreds of dismembered infants. This is strikingly similar to discoveries of thousands of dead babies discarded by modern abortion clinics. One scholar of the ancient Near East refers to infant sacrifice as "the Canaanite counterpart to abortion."[8]

Scripture condemns the shedding of innocent blood (Deut. 19:10; Prov. 6:17; Isa. 1:15; Jer. 22:17). While the killing of all innocent human beings is detestable, the Bible regards the killing of children as particularly heinous (Lev. 18:21; 20:1–5; Deut. 12:31). The prophets of Israel were outraged at the sacrifice of children by some of the Jews. They warned that it would result in the devastating judgment of God on their society (Jer. 7:30–34; Ezek. 16:20–21, 36–38; 20:31; compare 2 Kings 21:2–6 and Jer. 15:3–4).

Abortion and Church History

Christians throughout church history have affirmed with a united voice the humanity of the preborn child.[9] The second-century *Epistle of Barnabas* speaks of "killers of the child, who abort the mold of God." It treats the unborn child as any other human "neighbor" by saying, "You shall love your neighbor more than your own life. You shall not slay a child by abortion. You shall not kill that which has already been generated" (*Epistle of Barnabas* 19.5).

The *Didache*, a second-century catechism for young converts, states, "Do not murder a child by abortion or kill a newborn infant" (*Didache* 2.2). Clement of Alexandria maintained that "those who use abortifacient medicines to hide their fornication cause not only the outright murder of the fetus, but of the whole human race as well" (*Paedagogus* 2.10.96.1).

Defending Christians before Marcus Aurelius in A.D. 177, Athenagoras argued, "What reason would we have to commit murder when we say that women who induce abortions are murderers, and will have to give account of it to God? . . . The fetus in the womb is a living being and therefore the object of God's care" (*A Plea for the Christians* 35.137–138).

Tertullian said, "It does not matter whether you take away a life that is born, or destroy one that is coming to the birth. In both instances, destruction is murder" (*Apology* 9.4). Basil the Great affirmed, "Those who give abortifacients for the destruction of a child conceived in the womb are murderers themselves, along with those receiving the poisons" (*Canons* 188.2). Jerome called abortion "the murder of an unborn child" (*Letter to Eustochium* 22.13).

Augustine warned against the terrible crime of "the murder of an unborn child" (*On Marriage* 1.17.15). Origen, Cyprian, and Chrysostom were among the many other prominent theologians and church leaders who condemned abortion as the killing of children. New Testament scholar Bruce Metzger comments, "It is really remarkable how uniform and how pronounced was the early Christian opposition to abortion."[10]

Throughout the centuries, Roman Catholic leaders have consistently upheld the sanctity of human life. Likewise, Protestant reformer John Calvin followed both the Scriptures and the historical position of the church when he affirmed:

> The fetus, though enclosed in the womb of its mother, is already a human being and it is a most monstrous crime to rob it of the life which it has not yet begun to enjoy. If it seems more horrible to kill a man in his own house than in a field, because a man's house is his place of most secure refuge, it ought surely to be deemed more atrocious to destroy a fetus in the womb before it has come to light.[11]

Modern theologians with a strong biblical orientation have normally agreed that abortion is the killing of a child. Dietrich Bonhoeffer, who lost his life standing against the murder of the innocent in Germany, argued that abortion is "nothing but murder."[12]

Karl Barth stated, "The unborn child is from the very first a child . . . it is a man and not a thing, not a mere part of the mother's body. . . . Those who live by mercy will always be disposed to practice mercy, especially to a human being which is so dependent on the mercy of others as the unborn child."[13]

In the last few decades it has become popular for certain theologians and ministers to be pro-abortion. The Religious Coalition for Abortion Rights, for instance, has adopted the motto, "Prayerfully Pro-Choice," and pro-choice advocates point to it as proof that conscientious Christians can be pro-choice. Yet the arguments set forth by such advocates are shallow, inconsistent, and violate the most basic principles of biblical interpretation. Their arguments are clearly read into the biblical texts rather than derived from them.[14]

The "Christian" pro-choice position is nothing more than an accommodation to modern secular beliefs, and it flies in the face of the Bible and the historical position of the church. If the church is to be the church, it must challenge and guide the morality of society, not mirror it.

The Bible and The Children

Even if church history were unclear on the matter, the Bible is very clear. Every child in the womb has been created by God, and He has laid out a plan for that child's life. Furthermore, Christ loves that child and proved it by becoming like him—He spent nine months in His mother's womb. Finally, Christ died for that child, showing how precious He considers him to be.

Christ's disciples failed to understand how valuable children were to Him, and they rebuked those who tried to bring them near Him (Luke 18:15–17). But Jesus called the children to Him and said, "Let the little children come to me." He did not consider attention to children a distraction from His kingdom business, but an integral part of it.

The biblical view of children is that they are a blessing and gift from the Lord (Ps. 127:3–5). Society is treating children more and more as liabilities. We must learn to see them as God does—"He defends the cause of the fatherless and the widow, and loves the alien, giving him food and clothing" (Deut. 10:18). Furthermore, we must act toward them as God commands us to act:

> Defend the cause of the weak and fatherless;
>   maintain the rights of the poor and oppressed.
> Rescue the weak and needy;
>   deliver them from the hand of the wicked.
>   (Ps. 82:3–4)

As we intervene on behalf of His littlest children, let's realize it is Christ Himself for whom we intervene (Matt. 25:40).

Appendix 2

Biblical Passages Relevant to Life Issues

Note: Emphases are the author's.

1. *Life begins in the womb.*

"The *babies* [Jacob and Esau] jostled each other within her [Rebekah]" (Gen. 25:22).

> *Your hands shaped me and made me.*
>   Will you now turn and destroy me?
> Remember that *you molded me like clay.*
>   Will you now turn me to dust again?
> Did you not pour me out like milk
>   and curdle me like cheese,
> *clothe me with skin and flesh*
>   *and knit me together with bones and sinews*?
> You gave me life and showed me kindness,
>   and *in your providence watched over my spirit.* (Job 10:8–12)

> For you created my inmost being;
>   *you knit me together in my mother's womb.*
> I praise you because I am fearfully and wonderfully made. . . .
> My frame was not hidden from you
>   when I was made in the secret place,
>   when I was woven together in the depths of the earth.
> *Your eyes saw my unformed body;*
>   all the days ordained for me were written in your book
>   before one of them came to be. (Ps. 139:13–16)

> Surely I was sinful at birth;
>   *sinful from the time my mother conceived me.*
>> (Ps. 51:5) Note: Only a person can have a sin nature. David's statement clearly shows that he was a person at the point of conception.

> *Before I formed you in the womb I knew you,*
>> before you were born I set you apart;
>> I appointed you as a prophet to the nations. (Jer. 1:5)

"His mother Mary . . . was found to be *with child* through the Holy Spirit . . . [the angel said] *'what is conceived in her is from the Holy Spirit'* " (Matt. 1:18–20).

"But the angel said to [Mary]. . . . 'You will be *with child* and give birth to a son, and you are to give him the name Jesus. . . . The Holy Spirit will come upon you, and the power of the Most High will overshadow you. So the holy one to be born will be called the Son of God'" (Luke 1:30–31, 35).

Summary of Luke 1:39–44: After the angel left, Mary "hurried" (v. 39) to get to Elizabeth. Unborn John the Baptist (in his sixth month after conception) responded to the presence of unborn Jesus inside Mary. Allowing for travel time, Jesus was no more than eight to ten days beyond conception when they arrived. Implantation doesn't begin until six days after conception and isn't complete until twelve. *Most likely Jesus was not yet fully implanted in his mother's womb when unborn John responded to his presence.*

"The Word became flesh and made his dwelling among us. We have seen his glory, the glory of the One and Only, who came from the Father, full of grace and truth" (John 1:14).

When did God's Son leave heaven and come to earth? When and where did the Word become flesh? Ninety-nine percent of Christians will say "in Bethlehem," but that is wrong. Christ became flesh when the Holy Spirit conceived a child in Mary—at Nazareth, nine months before she traveled to Bethlehem. It is basic Christian doctrine that Christ became flesh at the moment the Holy Spirit overshadowed Mary, at the moment of fertilization. He became human at the exact point all others become human, the point of conception.

2. God is Creator and Owner of all people—they belong to Him, not others.

"So God created man in his own image, in the image of God he created him; male and female he created them" (Gen. 1:27).

Know that the LORD Himself is God:
It is He who has made us, and not we ourselves;
We are His people and the sheep of His pasture. (Ps. 100:3 NASB)

"For every living soul belongs to me, the father as well as the son" (Ezek. 18:4).

"Do you not know that your body is a temple of the Holy Spirit, who is in you, whom you have received from God? You are not your own; you were bought at a price. Therefore honor God with your body" (1 Cor. 6:19–20).

3. God has exclusive prerogatives over human life and death.

See now that I myself am He!
    There is no god besides me.
I put to death and I bring to life,
    I have wounded and I will heal,
        and no one can deliver out of my hand. (Deut. 32:39)

"The LORD brings death and makes alive; he brings down to the grave and raises up" (1 Sam. 2:6).

"You shall not commit murder" (Exod. 20:13). *Note: Murder is unjustified killing; in some cases God specifically delegates to men the right to kill (e.g., capital punishment, self-defense, just war).*

"And for your lifeblood I will surely demand an accounting. . . . And from each man, too, *I will demand an accounting for the life of his fellow man*" (Gen. 9:5).

"If men who are fighting hit a pregnant woman and she gives birth prematurely but there is no serious injury, the offender must be fined whatever the woman's husband demands and the court allows. But if there is serious injury, you are to take life for life, eye for eye, tooth for tooth, hand for hand, foot for foot, burn for burn, wound for wound, bruise for bruise" (Exod. 21:22–25).

"Nothing in all creation is hidden from God's sight. Everything is uncovered and laid bare before the eyes of him to whom we must give account" (Heb. 4:13).

4. God hates the shedding of innocent blood.

"*Do not give any of your children to be sacrificed* to Molech, for you must not profane the name of your God. I am the LORD" (Lev. 18:21).

"The LORD said . . . 'Any Israelite or any alien living in Israel who gives any of his children [as a sacrifice] to Molech must be put to death. The people of the community are to stone him. . . . *by giving his children to Molech, he has defiled my sanctuary and profaned my holy name.* . . . If the people of the community *close their eyes* when that man gives one of his children to Molech . . . I will set my face against that man and his family and will cut off from their people both him and all who follow him' " (Lev. 20:1–5).

"Do this *so that innocent blood will not be shed in your land,* which the LORD your God is giving you as your inheritance, and *so that you will not be guilty of bloodshed*" (Deut. 19:10).

"Surely these things [destruction by invading armies] happened to Judah according to the LORD's command, in order to remove them from his presence *because of the sins of Manasseh and all he had done, including the shedding of innocent blood.* For *he filled Jerusalem with innocent blood,* and the LORD was not willing to forgive" (2 Kings 24:3–4).

"The LORD said, 'What have you done? Listen! *Your brother's blood cries out to me from the ground*' " (Gen. 4:10).

> For God will deliver the needy who cry out,
> the afflicted who have no one to help.
> He will take pity on the weak and the needy
> and save the needy from death.
> He will rescue them from oppression and violence,
> for *precious is their blood in his sight.* (Ps. 72:12–14)

> There are six things the LORD hates,
> seven that are detestable to him:
> haughty eyes,
> a lying tongue,
> *hands that shed innocent blood* . . . (Prov. 6:16–17)

"Therefore as surely as I live, declares the Sovereign LORD, I will give you over to bloodshed and it will pursue you. *Since you did not hate bloodshed, bloodshed will pursue you*" (Ezek. 35:6).

5. God has a special love for children.

"See that you do not look down on one of these little ones. For I tell you that their angels in heaven always see the face of my Father in heaven" (Matt. 18:10).

"But Jesus called the children to him and said, 'Let the little children come to me, and do not hinder them, for the kingdom of God belongs to such as these'" (Luke 18:16).

"Your Father in heaven is not willing that any of these little ones should be lost" (Matt. 18:14).

Sons are a heritage from the LORD,
    children a reward from him. (Ps. 127:3)

Talking Points for Communicating the Pro-Life Message

Know Your Audience and Be Prepared

Tailor your conversation or presentation to your audience so that you're speaking to them, not to yourself.

Realize the vested interests, denial, and rationalization surrounding this issue. Many of the people you speak with have had abortions, recommended them, paid for them, or driven their girlfriend, wife, or daughter to get one. They have personal reasons for not wanting to believe abortion kills children.

Realize the average person's saturation and indoctrination with media propaganda. They have been conditioned to believe pro-lifers are anti-women, anti-choice, religious fanatics.

Do your homework. The success of the pro-choice position is dependent upon diverting attention *from* the central facts. Yours is dependent on drawing attention *to* them. You *must* know what you're talking about.

Present the facts logically, clearly, and succinctly, citing credible sources (secular whenever possible). For a more detailed refutation of the pro-choice position, see my book *ProLife Answers to ProChoice Arguments*.

Make the Pro-Life Case Clearly, Thoughtfully, and Accurately

Appeal to their curiosity and open-mindedness to hear a suppressed and politically incorrect viewpoint. (Pro-choice is the status quo, establishment position. Pro-life is the radical, counter-culture position.)

Surprise your audience. Don't fit the anti-abortion stereotype. Don't be negative or defensive; insist on letting the truth speak for itself. The evidence is on your side; don't make it ineffective by being a jerk.

Be rational and calm. Give the facts and let listeners develop their own emotions based on them. (Don't overwhelm people with *your* emotions. Don't go ballistic in a debate, as the other side often does. People who are listening will see which side is angry and irrational and which is calm and logical.)

Be prepared for straw man and ad hominem arguments, but don't use them yourself. When the facts aren't on their side, people have nothing left to do but distort issues and call names. This is inappropriate and unloving, and it is also extremely ineffective.

Be sensitive to the spiritual needs of your audience. Look and pray for heart change, not just head change. (Though head change can happen—people *can* change their minds about abortion, slavery, and other moral and social evils without embracing Christ as their Savior.)

Surprise Them and Get Their Attention

"Pro-choice is a meaningless term. Proof: I'm pro-choice. And you're not. I'm pro-choice about jobs, clothes, cars, schools, seat belts, smoking, etc. You're anti-choice about rape, kidnapping, assault, theft, and child molesting (and possibly even seat belts and smoking). Aren't you?"

"Let's not talk about "choice" as if that is the issue, let's talk about abortion. Then we can figure out whether we should defend people's right to choose abortion (like eating habits and clothing tastes) or oppose people's right to choose it (like rape and child abuse)."

"I don't believe in unwanted children. I just believe the solution is to want them, not kill them."

"I'm committed to women's rights. Like Susan B. Anthony and other pioneer feminists, I believe abortion is harmful and demeaning to women. In fact, abortion has become the primary method across the globe of eliminating unwanted females. Abortion is a means for irresponsible men to exploit women, using them sexually, then leaving them alone with the devastating physical and psychological consequences."

Ask Them Questions That Will Make Them Think (Sometimes for the First Time)

"You say you want to be called pro-choice, not pro-abortion. Why? What's wrong with abortion?" (The only good reason for feeling bad about abortion—that it kills an innocent child—should compel you to be against *others* doing it also. You should either say it's fine, or oppose it, but you can't logically do both.)

"See this ultrasound/intrauterine picture of a live unborn at eight weeks (at the time of an early abortion)? What does that look like? (Eye.) That? (Fingers.) That? (Mouth.) That? (Nose.)" Don't tell them. Let *them* answer. Then point out what they said.

"This baby has a measurable heartbeat at twenty-one days and brainwaves at forty days, before the earliest abortions. What do you call it when there is no longer a heartbeat or brainwaves? (Death.) What do you call it when there *is* a heartbeat and brainwaves? (Life.) What does abortion do? (Kills a living baby.)"

"This unborn baby is to a born infant what a born infant is to a toddler (younger and smaller). Do you think it would be more legitimate to kill an unwanted infant than a toddler just because he's younger and smaller?"

"If abortion isn't fundamentally different than other surgeries, like root canals and tonsillectomies, why are there so many post-abortion support groups and hundreds of thousands of women getting counseling and therapy related to their abortions? Do you know of any post-root canal counseling and support groups?"

"Why do you think it bothers you to see pictures of an abortion more than pictures of root canals or open-heart surgery? What's the difference?"

"Which side in the debate is cruel? The one that shows pictures of dead babies while opposing their killing, or the one that opposes showing the pictures but defends their killing?"

"You say the unborn is part of the mother's body? If that's true, then every pregnant woman has two hearts, two brains, two different genetic codes, two sets of fingers with different fingerprints, two heads, two noses, four eyes, two blood types, and two skeletal systems. And half the time she also has testicles and a penis."

"You *do* know the 'fetus' is a child, correct? When your friend says 'I'm carrying a child,' you don't disagree with her, do you?"

"You say abortion is legal, so we shouldn't oppose it. Did you know people said exactly the same about slavery and the mistreatment of Jews in Nazi Germany?"

"Abortion in the case of handicap? After they're born, we say they're precious and the family learns so much from them. We cheer them on in the Special Olympics. So before they're born why do we say, 'We don't want them; let's kill them while we can'? Isn't that hypocrisy, prejudice, and intolerance?"

"Abortion in the case of rape? Rape is never the fault of the child—why punish *her*? Don't you believe a child is a child, regardless of any bad thing her father did to someone? Besides, abortion is not a therapy, it's a *trauma* on a woman who has already undergone the trauma of rape. If you found out your best friend was the 'product of rape' would you think she deserved to die?"

"You say pro-lifers don't really care about the women, or the children once they're born? In fact, pro-life pregnancy centers providing free tests, care, classes, counseling, materials, and housing comprise the single largest grassroots volunteer movement in history. Countless pro-lifers adopt, open their homes, and volunteer to help children after they're born. The other side gets rich selling abortions. Whose motives should be suspect?"

"Will you read this carefully researched book or listen to this presentation? Will you look at the actual ultrasound images of living unborn children, or look at the photos or videos of abortion? If not, why not? Are you choosing to censor this side of the debate from your own consideration? I'll be glad to read anything you have for me from the other side. Let's read each other's material and talk about it honestly. Can we agree to follow the evidence wherever it leads?"

About the Author

Randy Alcorn is founder of Eternal Perspective Ministries (EPM), a nonprofit ministry dedicated to teaching principles of God's Word and assisting the church in ministering to the unreached, unfed, unborn, uneducated, unreconciled, and unsupported people around the world. His ministry focus is communicating the strategic importance of using our earthly time, money, possessions, and opportunities to invest in need-meeting ministries that count for eternity. He accomplishes this by analyzing, teaching, and applying biblical truth.

Before starting EPM in 1990, Randy served as a pastor for fourteen years. He holds degrees in theology and biblical studies and has taught on the adjunct faculties of Multnomah University and Western Seminary in Portland, Oregon.

Randy has written more than forty books, including the bestsellers *Courageous, Heaven, The Treasure Principle*, and the Gold Medallion winner *Safely Home*. His books in print exceed seven million and have been translated into more than thirty languages. Randy has written for many magazines including EPM's quarterly issues-oriented *Eternal Perspectives*. He is active daily on Facebook and Twitter, has been a guest on more than seven hundred radio, television, and online programs including *Focus on the Family, FamilyLife Today, Revive Our Hearts, The Bible Answer Man*, and *The Resurgence*.

Randy resides in Gresham, Oregon, with his wife, Nanci, and golden retriever, Maggie Grace. They have two married daughters, Karina and Angela, and are the proud grandparents of five grandsons—Jake, Matthew, Ty, Jack, and David. Randy enjoys hanging out with his family, biking, tennis, research, reading, and traveling.

Connect with Randy online

Facebook: www.facebook.com/randyalcorn
Twitter: www.twitter.com/randyalcorn
Blog: www.epm.org/blog

Eternal Perspective Ministries

39085 Pioneer Blvd., Suite 206
Sandy, OR 97055
503-668-5200
Toll Free Order Line: 1-877-376-4567
Email: info@epm.org
Website: www.epm.org
Facebook: www.facebook.com/EPMinistries
Twitter: www.twitter.com/epmorg

Notes

Chapter 1: Why Talk about Abortion?

1. "Gallup: 72% of Teens Say Abortion Wrong," WorldNetDaily, November 24, 2003, http://www.wnd.com/?s=gallup+teens+say+abortion+.

2. Lydia Saad, "The New Normal on Abortion: Americans More 'Pro-Life,'" Gallup Politics, May 14, 2010, http://www.gallup.com/poll/128036/New-Normal-Abortion-Americans-Pro-Life.aspx.

3. Steven Ertelt, "Gallup Poll: Americans Want All or Most Abortions Illegal," LifeNews, May 23, 2011, http://www.lifenews.com/2011/05/23/gallup-poll-americans-want-all-or-most-abortions-illegal/.

4. *The Advocate*, Live Action, http://liveaction.org/files/advocate/advocate6.pdf.

5. David Schmidt, "Polling Data: America's Youth Becoming Pro-Life," *Live Action* blog, May 15, 2010, http://liveaction.org/blog/polling-data-americas-youth-becoming-pro-life/.

6. Live Action, "The Mona Lisa Project," accessed December 2011, http://liveaction.org/monalisa.

7. See www.standupgirl.com.

8. Guttmacher Institute, "Facts on Induced Abortion in the United States," August 2011, http://guttmacherinstitute.org/pubs/fb_induced_abortion.html.

9. Ibid.

10. Lydia Saad, "Americans Still Split along 'Pro-Choice,' 'Pro-Life' Lines," Gallup Politics, May 23, 2011, http://www.gallup.com/poll/147734/Americans-Split-Along-Pro-Choice-Pro-Life-Lines.aspx.

11. Rachel K. Jones, Lawrence B. Finer, and Susheela Singh, "Characteristics of U.S. Abortion Patients, 2008," Guttmacher Institute, May 2010, http://www.guttmacher.org/pubs/US-Abortion-Patients.pdf.

12. Randy Alcorn, *ProLife Answers to ProChoice Arguments* (Sisters, OR: Multnomah, 2000).

Chapter 2: Pro-Woman or Pro-Child?

1. Lydia Saad, "Americans Still Split along 'Pro-Choice,' 'Pro-life' Lines," Gallup Politics, May 23, 2011, http://www.gallup.com/poll/147734/

Americans-Split-Along-Pro-Choice-Pro-Life-Lines.aspx. See also "Gallup Finds Two-Thirds of Americans Believe Abortion Is Morally Wrong," LifeSiteNews, June 3, 2003, www.lifesite.net/ldn/2003/jun/03060308.html.

2. Paul Swope, "Abortion: A Failure to Communicate," *First Things*, April 1998, 31–35.

Chapter 3: Are the Unborn Really Human Beings?

1. Planned Parenthood, Q&A with Dr. Cullins, accessed February 18, 2012, http://www.plannedparenthood.org/health-topics/ask-dr-cullins/cullins-ec-5360.htm.

2. Subcommittee on Separation of Powers to Senate Judiciary Committee S-158, Report, 97th Cong., 1st Session, 1981.

3. Ibid.

4. Alexander Tsiaras, *From Conception to Birth: A Life Unfolds* (New York: Doubleday, 2002). View his video, "Conception to Birth—Visualized!", 2010, http://www.ted.com/talks/alexander_tsiaras_conception_to_birth_visualized.html.

5. "Life Begins at Fertilization," December 2011, http://www.princeton.edu/~Prolife/articles/embryoquotes2.html.

6. *Missouri Revised Statutes*, chap., "Laws in Force and Construction of Statutes," § 1.205, August 28, 2003, http://www.moga.mo.gov/statutes/C000-099/0010000205.htm.

7. Frederick S. Jaffe (Vice President of Planned Parenthood–World Population), "Memorandum to Bernard Berelson (President, Population Council) found in 'Activities Relevant to the Study of Population Policy for the U.S.'" (March 11, 1969), *A Family Planning Perspectives Special Supplement* (New York: Planned Parenthood–World Population, 1970), cited at US Coalition for Life, http://uscl.info/edoc/doc.php?doc_id=49&action=inline.

8. The Association of Pro-Life Physicians, "When Does Life Begin?," accessed August 6, 2012, http://Prolifephysicians.org/lifebegins.htm.

9. *Roe v. Wade*, 410 U.S. (1973).

10. David Boonin, *A Defense of Abortion* (New York: Cambridge University Press, 2002), xiii–xiv, cited in Lita Cosner, "When Does the Unborn Baby Feel Pain?" July 22, 2010, http://creation.com/unborn-baby-fetal-pain-abortion.

11. R. Houwink, *Data: Mirrors of Science* (New York: American Elsevier, 1970), 104–90.

12. Chemicals designated A, C, T & G form the basis for all DNA with variations in the order of the chemicals resulting in cell specialization and tissue differentiation. www.ornl.gov/sci/techresources/Human_Genome/faq/faqs1.shtml.

13. Lennart Nilsson, "Drama of Life before Birth," *Life*, April 30, 1965.

14. "The Facts of Life" (Norcross, GA: Human Development Resource Council), 2.

15. Vincent J. Collins, "Fetal Pain and Abortion: The Medical Evidence," *Studies in Law and Medicine* (Chicago: Americans United for Life, 1984), 6–7.

16. See "The War over Fetal Rights," *Newsweek,* June 9, 2003, 40–47.

17. These are well-established scientific facts. See, e.g., Landrum Shettles and David Rorvik, *Rites of Life* (Grand Rapids: Zondervan, 1983), 41–66.

18. Justin Taylor, "Sticker Shock," *World,* January 17, 2004, 43.

Chapter 4: What's the Difference between Egg, Sperm, and Fetus?

1. Leonide M. Tanner, ed., "Developing Professional Parameters: Nursing and Social Work Roles in the Care of the Induced Abortion Patient," *Clinical Obstetrics and Gynecology* 14 (December 1971): 1271.

2. Paul Marx, *The Death Peddlers: War on the Unborn* (Collegeville, MN: St. John's University Press, 1971), 21.

3. *Feminists for Life Debate Handbook* (Kansas City, MO: Feminists for Life of America, n.d.), 3.

4. Carl Sagan and Ann Druyan, "Abortion: Is It Possible to Be 'Pro-life' and 'Pro-Choice'?" *Parade,* April 22, 1990, 4.

5. *The First Nine Months* (Colorado Springs: Focus on the Family, 2008), 7.

6. *Preview of a Birth* (Norcross, GA: Human Development Resource Center, 1991), 4.

7. Scott Klusendorf, *The Case for Life: Equipping Christians to Engage the Culture* (Westchester, IL: Crossway, 2009).

8. See Scott Klusendorf, "Harvesting the Unborn: The Ethics of Embryo Stem Cell Research," Stand to Reason, accessed August 6, 2012, http://www.str.org/site/DocServer/harvest.pdf?docID=150.

9. "Who's Who—Stem Cell Organizations," StemCellResources, accessed December 9, 2011, http://www.stemcellresources.org/who_orgs.html.

10. "Deadline Extended for Comment to NIH on Stem Cells Harvesting," *Pro-life Infonet,* January 31, 2000.

11. What Are Embryonic Stem Cells?" National Institutes of Health, Stem Cell Basics, accessed December 2, 2011, http://stemcells.nih.gov/info/basics/basics3.asp.

12. Theodor Geisel, *Horton Hears a Who!* (New York: Random House, 1954), 47.

13. S. Noggle et al., *Nature* 478 (2011): 70–75.

14. Thomas W. Hilgers, Dennis J. Horan, and David Mall, eds., *New Perspectives on Human Abortion* (Frederick, MD: University Publications of America/Aletheia Books, 1981), 351. See NaPro Technology, http://www.naprotechnology.com/.

15. Stephanie Pappas, "Why Mississippi's 'Personhood' Law Could Outlaw Birth Control," *Live Science*, November 7, 2011, http://www.livescience.com/16917-mississippi-personhood-birth-control.html.

16. Warren M. Hern, "Did I Violate the Partial-Birth Abortion Ban? A Doctor Ponders a New Era of Prosecution," *Slate: Medical Examiner*, October 22, 2003, http://www.slate.msn.com/id/2090215.

Chapter 5: Is an Unborn Child Part of the Mother's Body?

1. Mortimer J. Adler, *Haves without Have-Nots: Essays for the 21st Century on Democracy and Socialism* (New York: Macmillan, 1991), 210.

2. Tanya Albert, "Fetus Determined to Be Part of Mother's Body," *American Medical News*, June 2–9, 2003, http://www.ama-assn.org/amednews/2003/06/02/prsc0602.htm.

3. For a graphic overview of this process, see University of Pennsylvania, Perelman School of Medicine, http://www.med.upenn.edu/meded/public/berp/overview/BV_1.html?6.

4. Y. Kudo *et al.*, "Indoleamine 2,3-Dioxygenase: Distribution and Function in the Developing Human Placenta, *Journal of Reproductive Immunology* 61, no. 2 (2004): 87–98.

5. David Pallister, "British Ice Skater Gives Birth Two Days after Fatal Brain Haemorrhage," *The Guardian*, January 12, 2009, http://www.guardian.co.uk/society/2009/jan/13/ice-skater-soliman-birth; see also "Brain-Dead Mother Gives Birth to Boy in Saudi Arabia," Al Bawa, June 28, 2011, http://www.albawaba.com/brain-dead-mother-gives-birth-boy-s-arabia-380588.

6. Michael Harrison, MD, "Minimally Invasive Fetoscopic Surgery," March 9, 2009, http://www.youtube.com/watch?v=7mDXqGTT0Uo.

7. Michael Clancy, *Hand of Hope, The Story behind the Picture* (Createspace [self-published], 2011), ISBN 1463755724.

8. See Michael Clancy, "The Story behind the Picture," http://michaelclancy.com/?page_id=94.

9. Chuck Colson, "Life-and-Death Decisions: Praying for the Supremes," *BreakPoint*, April 25, 2000, http://www.breakpoint.org/commentaries/4409-life-and-death-decisions.

10. The Innocent Child Protection Act (HR 4888), July 12, 2000. See National Right to Life, Press Release, "U.S. House Passes Ban on State Execution of 'Child in Utero,'" July 25, 2000, http://www.nrlc.org/Federal/ICPA/housestateexecution.htm.

11. HR 1997 was passed by a Senate roll call vote of 61 to 38, March 25, 2004.

Chapter 6: What Do the Pictures Tell Us?

1. Madeline Nash, "Inside the Womb," *Time*, November, 11, 2002, 68–77; Debra Rosenberg, "The War over Fetal Rights," *Newsweek*, June 9, 2003, 40–51.

2. Sarah Kliff, "The Prenatal Problem," *Newsweek*, January 18, 2010.

3. R. Albert Mohler, Jr., "First Person: Who's Afraid of the Fetus?," Baptist Press, 2-14-2005, http://www.bpnews.net/bpcolumn.asp?ID=1725.

4. Thomas Glessner, *Emerging Brave New World* (Crane, MO: Anomalos Publishing, 2008).

5. Jennifer Kabbany, "Abortion vs. Ultrasound," *Washington Times*, October 29, 2003.

6. Family Research Council Ultrasound Policy, Jeanne Monahan, "Why Ultrasounds Are Important," July 2010, http://downloads.frc.org/EF/EF10G59.pdf, based on "Patient Characteristics and Attitudes about Viewing an Ultrasound in a Pregnancy Resource Center: Chicago (a) and Boston (b) Studies," Z. Harry Piotrowski et al., American Public Health Association, 132 Annual Meeting. Washington, DC, November 9, 2004.

7. Audrey Stout (Marietta, GA) e-mail to Randy Alcorn, February 12, 2000.

8. *Life*, August 1990.

9. Lennart Nilsson, *A Child Is Born* (New York: Delacorte Press, 1977).

10. "Ultrasound Images Used in Ohio Abortion Hearing," Christian Broadcasting Network News, March 3, 2011, http://www.cbn.com/cbnnews/us/2011/March/Ultrasound-Images-Used-in-Ohio-Abortion-Hearing/, click on video.

11. For photographic evidence on abortion, see The Center for BioEthical Reform, http://www.abortionno.org/, also The Abortion Truth, http://www.abortiontruth.com/pictures.htm

12. "Planned Parenthood Admits Infanticide," March 11, 2009, http://www.youtube.com/watch?v=4ubrw80RbEQ&feature=related; also The Mona Lisa Project at Live Action, http://liveaction.org/media/download-live-action-videos; see also "180 the Movie" by filmmaker Ray Comfort, September 21, 2011, http://www.youtube.com/watch?v=7y2KsU_dhwI.

13. Warren Hern, "Operative Procedures and Technique," *Abortion Practice* (Boulder, CO: Alpenglo Graphics, 1990), 154.

14. Naomi Wolf, "Our Bodies, Our Souls," *The New Republic*, October 16, 1995.

15. The Center for Bioethical Reform, www.abortionno.org.

16. "Negative Psychological Impact of Sonography in Abortion," *ObGyn News*, February 15–28, 1986.

17. Milagos Rivera-Sanchez and Paul H. Gates, Jr., "Abortion on the Air: Broadcasters and Indecent Political Advertising," *Federal Communications Law*

Journal 46, no. 2 (1993–1994), http://www.law.indiana.edu/fclj/pubs/v46/no2/gates.html.

18. Scott Whitlock, "Barbara Walters: It's 'Heartbreaking' to Force Women to View an Ultrasound before an Abortion," Media Research Center, February 9, 2012, http://www.mrc.org/node/39085.

19. Adam Cohen, "The Next Abortion Battleground: Fetal Heartbeats," *Time*, October 17, 2011.

20. Canadian Centre for Bioethical Reform, "The New Abortion Caravan," http://www.unmaskingchoice.ca/caravan, accessed 9-24-2012.

21. Lynn Marie Morgan, *Icons of Life: a Cultural History of Human Embryos* (Berkeley and Los Angeles: University of California Press, 2009), 221.

Chapter 7: What Makes a Human Life "Meaningful"?

1. Douglas Martin, "Dr. William Harrison, Defender of Abortion Rights, Dies at 75," *New York Times*, September 25, 2010.

2. Mary Fischer, "A New Look at Life," *Reader's Digest*, October 2003, 95–103.

3. Peter Singer, *Practical Ethics* (New York: Cambridge University Press, 1979).

4. Peter Singer, FAQ [Frequently Asked Questions], Princeton University, accessed December 6, 2011, http://www.princeton.edu/~psinger/faq.html, under "The Sanctity of Human Life."

5. Jim Newhall, cited in Maureen O'Hagan, "Cross Hairs to Bear," *Willamette Week*, May 3, 1995.

6. *Roe v. Wade*, 410 U.S. 113 (1973), 38.

7. Fox News, "Alabama Court's Wrongful Death Ruling Used to Recommend Abandoning 'Roe' Viability Argument," February 20, 2012, http://www.foxnews.com/politics/2012/02/20/alabama-courts-wrongful-death-ruling-used-to-recommend-abandoning-viability/.

8. Associated Press, cited in Christian Action Council's *Action Line*, March–April 1991.

9. "Babies' Language Learning Starts from the Womb," *Science Daily*, November 5, 2009; from Mampe et al., "Newborns' Cry Melody Is Shaped by Their Native Language," *Current Biology*, November 5, 2009, doi:10.1016/j.cub.2009.09.064.

10. David B. Chamberlain, "Introduction to Life before Birth," *Birth Psychology*, accessed December 6, 2011, http://birthpsychology.com/free-article/introduction-life-birth.

11. Sharon Begley, "Do You Hear What I Hear?," *Newsweek*, Special Summer Edition 1991, 12.

12. Ibid.

13. H. B. Valman and J. F. Pearson, "What the Fetus Feels." *British Medical Journal* 280, no. 6209 (January 26, 1980): 233–34.

14. "Baby's First Dreams: Sleep Cycles of the Fetus." *Science Daily,* April 14, 2009, http://www.sciencedaily.com/releases/2009/04/090413185734.htm.

15. Begley, "Do You Hear?," 14.

16. An abortion provider describes one late-term technique, see "The Truth about Abortion (Dilation and Extraction)," February 10, 2010, http://www.youtube.com/watch?v=Q6rqYUFfeMc.

17. Peter Singer, "Sanctity of Life or Quality of Life," *Pediatrics,* July 1983, 129.

18. Sylvia Nasar, "Princeton's New Philosopher Draws a Stir," New York Times, 4-10-1999, http://people.brandeis.edu/~teuber/singerdrawsastir.html, excerpted quote from Peter Singer, *Practical Ethics, 2nd ed.* (New York: Cambridge University Press, 1993); excerpted from Singer, *Practical Ethics, 2nd ed.* (New York: Cambridge University Press, 1993).

19. Charles Hartshorne, "Concerning Abortion: An Attempt at a Rational View," *Christian Century,* January 21, 1981, 42–45.

20. David Boonin, *A Defense of Abortion* (New York: Cambridge University Press, 2003), 5–9.

21. Cited in Liz Klimas, "Ethicists Argue in Favor of 'After-birth Abortions,' as Newborns Are 'Not Persons,' *The Blaze*, February 27, 2012, http://www.theblaze.com/stories/ethicists-argue-in-favor-of-after-birth-abortions-as-newborns-are-not-persons/.

22. Alberto Guibini & Francesca Minerva, Abstract "After Birth Abortion: Why Should the Baby Live?" *Journal of Medical Ethics,* http://jme.bmj .com/content/early/2012/03/01/medethics-2011-100411.full; also, Wesley J. Smith, "The 'Duty to Die' Advances," *Free Republic,* October 20, 2011, http://www.freerepublic.com/focus/f-news/2795716/posts.

23. *Feminists for Life Debate Handbook* (Kansas City, MO: Feminists for Life of America, n.d.), 9.

24. For a treatment of the biblical and ethical issues involved in euthanasia, see Randy Alcorn, "Euthanasia: Mercy or Murder?" 1986/January 14, 2010, www.epm.org/euthanas.html.

25. "Gov. Lamm Asserts Elderly, if Very Ill, Have 'Duty to Die,'" March 29, 1984, http://www.nytimes.com/1984/03/29/us/gov-lamm-asserts-elderly-if-very-ill-have-duty-to-die.html. Note that the *New York Times* editors add a November 23, 1993, addendum to the 1984 news article in which they cite Lamm's clarification of his statement.

26. C. Everett Koop, *Action Line: Christian Action Council Newsletter* 9, no. 5 (July 12, 1985), 3.

27. Quoted in George Will, *The Pursuit of Happiness and Other Sobering Thoughts* (New York: Harper Colophon, 1978), 62–63.

Chapter 8: Is Abortion Really a Women's Rights Issue?

1. Kate Michelman, quoted in *New York Times,* May 10, 1988.

2. Susan B. Anthony, *The Revolution,* 4(1):4, July 8,1869.

3. *Feminists for Life Debate Handbook* (Kansas City, MO: Feminists for Life of America, n.d.), 17

4. Rosemary Bottcher, "Feminism: Bewitched by Abortion," in *To Rescue the Future,* ed. Dave Andrusko (New York: Life Cycle Books, 1983).

5. Angi Becker Stevens, "The Hypocrisy of 'Informed Consent' Abortion Laws," RH Reality Check: Reproductive & Sexual Health and Justice News, Analysis and Commentary blog, April 15, 2011, http://www.rhrealitycheck. org/blog/2011/04/14/hypocrisy-informed-consent.

6. Planned Parenthood Federation of America, *Annual Report* 2009–2010, June 30, 2010, 6, http://issuu.com/actionfund/docs/ppfa_financials_ 2010_122711_web_vf?mode=window&viewMode=doublePage.

7. "Planned Parenthood Aids Pimp's Underage Sex Ring," Live Action blog, February 1, 2011, http://liveaction.org/blog/planned-parenthood-aids-sex-ring-full-footage/. Susan K. Livio, "Englewood Health Clinic Faces NJ Inquiry after Undercover Video," NJ.com, February 3, 2011, http://www.nj.com/ news/index.ssf/2011/02/englewood_health_clinic_faces.html.

8. Devlin Dwyer, "Abortion Activists Attempt to Discredit Planned Parenthood with Second Video," ABC News, February 4, 2011, http://abcnews. go.com/Politics/activists-targeting-planned-parenthood-release-undercover-video/story?id=12831614.

9. Frank James, "Planned Parenthood: Budget Fight about Us, Not Abortion Funding," *NPR: It's All Politics,* NPR blog, April 8, 2011, http://www.npr. org/blogs/itsallpolitics/2011/04/08/135236230/planned-parenthood-budget-fight-about-us-not-abortion-money.

10. "New Planned Parenthood Annual Report Confirms Abortions Total 91% of Pregnancy Services," *Live Action blog,* January 3, 2012, http://liveaction. org/blog/new-planned-parenthood-annual-report-confirms-abortion-makes-up-91-of-pregnancy-related-services/.

11. Charmaine Yoest, "Five Truths about Planned Parenthood," *National Review,* April, 26, 2011, http://www.nationalreview.com/articles/265590/ five-truths-about-planned-parenthood-charmaine-yoest.

12. Serrin Foster, "The Feminist Case against Abortion," *The Commonwealth* (September 13, 1999), www.feministsforlife.org/news/commonw.htm.

13. Susan B. Anthony, *The Revolution,* July 8, 1869, 4.

14. Mattie Brinkerhoff, *The Revolution,* April 9, 1868, 215–16.

15. Guy M. Condon, "You Say Choice, I Say Murder," *Christianity Today,* June 24, 1991, 22; "Abortion and the Early Feminists," BBC Ethics Guide,

accessed December 8, 2011, http://www.bbc.co.uk/ethics/abortion/mother/early.shtml.

16. "A Short history of the E.R.A.," *The Phyllis Schlafly Report*, Eagle Forum, accessed December 8, 2011, http://www.eagleforum.org/psr/1986/sept86/psrsep86.html.

17. "Eugenics without birth control seemed to me a house built upon sands . . . The eugenicists wanted to shift the birth-control emphasis from less children for the poor to more children for the rich. We went back of that and sought to stop the multiplication of the unfit." Margaret Sanger, quoted in Linda Gordon, *Woman's Body, Woman's Right* (New York: Grossman, 1976), 287, 278–79; or see Michael Perry, "The History of Planned Parenthood," *EWTN Global Catholic Network*, accessed December 8, 2011, http://www.ewtn.com/library/Prolife/pphistry.txt.

18. Margaret Sanger, "The Birth Control Review," https://www.lifedynamics.com/library/#birthcontrol; https://www.lifedynamics.com/library/#books.

19. Margaret Sanger, *Pivot of Civilization* (New York: Brentano's, 1922), 176.

20. Ibid., 177.

21. Ibid., 112, 116.

22. Ibid., 113.

23. Ibid., 115.

24. Havelock Ellis, "The World's Racial Problem," *Birth Control Review (BCR)*, October 1920, 14–16; Theodore Russell Robie, "Toward Race Betterment," *BCR*, April 1933, 93–95; Ernst Rudin, "Eugenic Sterilization: An Urgent Need," *BCR*, April 1933, 102–4.

25. Marvin Olasky, *Abortion Rites: A Social History of Abortion in America* (Wheaton, IL: Crossway, 1992), 256–57.

26. Ibid., 258.

27. Ibid., 259.

28. Ibid., 259–63, 277; Sanger, *Pivot of Civilization*, 116–17.

29. Sanger, *Pivot of Civilization*, 116–17.

30. Margaret Sanger, "Why the Woman Rebel?," *The Woman Rebel* 1, no. 1 (March 1914): 8, The Public Papers of Margaret Sanger, New York University, accessed December 8, 2011, http://www.nyu.edu/projects/sanger/webedition/app/documents/show.php?sangerDoc=420037.xml.

31. Elasah Drogin, *Margaret Sanger: Father of Modern Society* (CUL Publications, 1989), 11–13.

32. R. C. Sproul, *Abortion: A Rational Look at an Emotional Issue* (Colorado Springs: NavPress, 1990), 117–18.

33. Mary Ann Schaefer, quoted in Catherine and William Odell, *The First Human Right* (Toronto: Life Cycle Books, 1983), 39–40.

34. *The American Feminist*, Spring 2003, 14, 17.

35. "Abortion and Moral Beliefs: A Survey of American Opinion," conducted by the Gallup Organization (1991), 4–7.

36. John Willke, "The Real Woman's Movement," *National Right to Life News*, 14 December 1989, 3.

37. Condon, "You Say Choice," 23.

38. Alan B. Goldberg and Sean Dooley, "Disappearing Daughters: Women Pregnant with Girls Pressured into Abortions," December 9, 2011, http://abcnews.go.com/Health/women-pregnant-girls-pressured-abortions-india/story?id=15103950; see also Barb Lyons, "India: 50,000 Girls Become Victims of Abortion Monthly, LifeNews.com, December 20, 2011, http://www.lifenews.com/2011/12/20/india-50000-girls-become-victims-of-abortion-monthly/ to view a news clip; Ruchira Gupta, *Disappearing Daughters: The Tragedy of Female Fetocide* (Penguin Books India, 2007).

39. Stephen W. Mosher, "Sex-Selective Abortions Come Home," *National Review* Online, December 6, 2011, http://www.nationalreview.com/corner/284988/sex-selective-abortions-come-home-steven-w-mosher.

40. T. Hesketh and Z. W. Xing, "Abnormal Sex Ratios in Human Populations: Causes and Consequences," Proceedings of the National Academy of Sciences USA 103, no. 36 (September 5, 2006): 13271–75. Epub August 28, 2006.

41. "Women—An Endangered Species," *World Development Forum* 5, no. 21 (November 30, 1987): 1–2.

42. Claire Newell, "Abortions to Reduce Multiple Births on the Rise," *The Telegraph,* December 28, 2011, http://www.telegraph.co.uk/health/8981504/Abortions-to-reduce-multiple-births-on-the-rise.html.

43. Martin Beckford, "Abortion Risk Warning to Women Pregnant with Twins," *The Telegraph*, September 28, 2011, http://www.telegraph.co.uk/health/women_shealth/8792087/Abortion-risk-warning-to-women-pregnant-with-twins.html.

44. "Scientists Grow Sperm in Laboratory Dish," *The Telegraph*, January 2, 2012, http://www.telegraph.co.uk/health/healthnews/8988011/Scientists-grow-sperm-in-laboratory-dish.html.

45. "UNFPA Presented 'Prevalence and Reasons of Sex Selective Abortions in Armenia' Report," Public Radio of Armenia, December 19, 2011, http://www.armradio.am/eng/news/?part=soc&id=21628.

46. Mosher, "Sex-Selective Abortions Come Home"; see also Joel Kotkin, "How a Baby Bust Will Turn Asia's Tiger Toothless," New Geography, March 29, 2012, http://www.newgeography.com/content/002753-how-a-baby-bust-will-turn-asias-tigers-toothless.

47. Robert Stone, "Women Endangered Species in India," *The Oregonian*, March 14, 1989.

48. Jo McGowan, "In India They Abort Females," *Newsweek*, February 13, 1989.

49. Jeff Hays, "Preference for Boys and Missing Girls in China," updated October 2011, http://factsanddetails.com/china.php?itemid=126&catid=4& subcatid=15.

50. Wei Zing Zhu et al., "China's Excess Males, Sex Selective Abortion and One-Child Policy: Analysis of Data from 2005 National Intercensus Survey," *British Journal of Medicine*, April 9, 2009, http://www.bmj.com/content/338/ bmj.b1211.full.

51. *Medical World News,* December 1, 1975, 45; see also "Brave New Babies," *Newsweek,* February 1, 2004.

52. F. Moazam, "Feminist Discourse on Sex-Screening and Selective Abortion of Female Foetuses," *Bioethics* 18, no. 3 (June 2004): 205–20.

Chapter 9: Do We Have the Right to Choose What We Do with Our Bodies?

1. "When Abortion was Illegal," Section "Abortion: Facts at a Glance," (Planned Parenthood Federation of America); http://www.bullfrogfilms.com/ guides/wawguide.pdf, 10.

2. K. A. Kunkel, "Safe Haven Laws Focus on Abandoned Newborns and Their Mothers," *Journal of Pediatric Nursing 22, no. 5 (October 2007)*: 397–401, *see abstract at National Center for Biotechnology Information,* http://www.ncbi. nlm.nih.gov/pubmed/17889732.

3. Mary O'Brien Drum, "Meeting in the Radical Middle," *Sojourners,* November 1980, 23.

4. Nat Brandt, *The Town That Started the Civil War* (New York: Syracuse University Press, 1990); Thomas Clarkson, *Slavery and Commerce of the Human Species* (1788; repr., Miami, FL: Mnemosyne, 1969); Austin Willey, *The History of the Anti-Slavery Cause* (1886; repr., Miami, FL: Mnemosyne, 1969); Fergus M. Bordewich, *Bound for Canaan* (New York: HarperCollins, 2005).

Chapter 10: Does Our "Right to Privacy" Include Abortion?

1. US Holocaust Memorial Museum, Holocaust Encyclopedia, s.v. Euthanasia Program, accessed December 8, 2011, http://www.ushmm.org/wlc/en/ article.php?ModuleId=10005200.

2. See Robert Jay Lifton, *The Nazi Doctors: Medical Killing and the Psychology of Genocide* (New York: Basic Books, 1986).

3. Edwin Black, "The Horrifying American Roots of Nazi Eugenics," *San Francisco Chronicle*, reprinted at George Mason University's History News Network, November 25, 2003, http://hnn.us/articles/1796.html.

4. See www.teen-aid.org/Links.htm; www.abstinencedu.com; Abstinence and Marriage Education Partnership, http://www.ampartnership.org/.

5. Mark Baker, "Men on Abortion," *Esquire*, March 1990, 114–25.

Chapter 11: Does Abortion Harm a Woman's Physical and Mental Health?

1. Serrin M. Foster, "Women Deserve Better than Abortion," *Respect Life*, 2003.

2. Quoted in Mary Meehan, "The Ex-Abortionists: Why They Quit," *Human Life Review* (Spring–Summer 2000), 12.

3. Ibid., 23.

4. Priscilla Coleman, "Abortion and Mental Health: Quantitative Synthesis and Analysis of Research Published 1995–2009," *British Journal of Psychiatry* 199 (September 2011): 180–86, http://bjp.rcpsych.org/content/199/3/180.abstract.

5. Jim Coyne, PhD, "More on Review Claiming Abortion Hurts Women's Mental Health," *Psychology Today blog*, November 15, 2011, http://www.psychologytoday.com/blog/the-skeptical-sleuth/201111/more-review-claiming-abortion-hurts-womens-mental-health.

6. Priscilla Coleman, "Re: Abortion and Mental Health," *British Journal of Psychiatry BJP Online*, November 17, 2011, http://bjp.rcpsych.org/content/199/3/180.abstract/reply#bjrcpsych_el_34290.

7. Joseph A. D'Agostino, "Abortion Causes Massive Mental Health Problems for Women," *Human Events*, January 30, 2006, http://www.humanevents.com/article.php?id=11966&keywords=abortion+ectopic+pregnancy.

8. Judith Lewis Herman, *Trauma and Recovery* (New York: Basic Books, 1992), 34; also, David C. Reardon, *Making Abortion Rare*, Acorn Books, 1996; excerpt, http://afterabortion.org/MAR/IGCHAP6.htm, fn 4).

9. For this and other studies, see Elliot Institute, www.afterabortion.org.

10. David C. Reardon, "Major Psychological Sequelae of Abortion" (Elliot Institute, 1997).

11. Susan Babbel, PhD, MFT, "Post Abortion Stress Syndrome (PASS)—Does It Exist?," *Psychology Today* blog, October 25, 2010, http://www.psychologytoday.com/blog/somatic-psychology/201010/post-abortion-stress-syndrome-pass-does-it-exist.

12. "Tearing Down the Wall," *LifeSupport*, Spring–Summer 1991,1–3. "Women Exploited by Abortion, Nancy Jo Mann's Story," from David Reardon, *Aborted Women, Silent No More*, posted by *United Families International blog*, April

14, 2009, http://unitedfamiliesinternational.wordpress.com/2009/04/14/women-exploited-by-abortion-nancyjo-mann%E2%80%99s-story.

13. See Randy Alcorn, *ProLife Answers to ProChoice Arguments (Sisters, OR: Multnomah, 2000)*, 118–20, 285–86.

14. Free information and counseling is available via Life Issues Institute, www.lifeissues.org/men/; also Abortion Is the Unchoice, http://theunchoice.org/men.htm; Silent No More Awareness, accessed January 4, 2012, http://www.silentnomoreawareness.org/resources/.

15. Angela Lanfranchi, MD, "The Science, Studies and Sociology of the Abortion Breast Cancer Link," *Association for Interdisciplinary Research in Values and Social Change, Research Bulletin* 18, no. 2 (Spring 2005), http://www.abortionbreastcancer.com/June2005.pdf.

16. Elizabeth Shadigian, MD, testimony before the Senate subcommittee on science, technology, and space's hearing to investigate the physical and psychological effects of abortion on women; cited in "Witnesses Ask U.S. Senate for Research into Side Effects of Abortion on Women," *Culture & Cosmos* 1, no. 30 (March 9, 2004).

17. Laura Blue, "Study Links Abortion and Premies," *Time,* December 18, 2007, citing the *Journal of Epidemiology and Community Health,* http://www.time.com/time/health/article/0,8599,1695927,00.html.

18. Brent Rooney and Byron C. Calhoun, MD, "Induced Abortion and Risk of Later Premature Births," *Journal of American Physicians and Surgeons* 8, no. 2 (Summer 2003), http://www.jpands.org/vol8no2/rooney.pdf.

19. Brent Rooney et al., "Does Induced Abortion Account for Racial Disparity in Preterm Births, and Violate the Nuremberg Code?," *Journal of American Physicians and Surgeons* 13, no. 4 (Winter 2008), http://www.jpands.org/vol13no4/rooney.pdf.

20. S. Linn, "The Relationship between Induced Abortion and Outcome of Subsequent Pregnancies," *American Journal of Obstetrics and Gynecology,* May 15, 1983, 136–40.

21. John A. Richardson and Geoffrey Dixon, "Effects of Legal Termination on Subsequent Pregnancy," *British Medical Journal* (1976): 1303–4.

22. B. Luke, *Every Pregnant Woman's Guide to Preventing Premature Birth* (New York: Times Books, 1995); E. Ring-Cassidy, *Woman's Health after Abortion* (Toronto: de Veber Institute, 2002).

23. M. E. Lloyd et al., "Effects of Methotrexate on Pregnancy, Fertility and Lactation," *QJM* 92, no. 10 (1999): 551–63, accessed December 9, 2011, http://qjmed.oxfordjournals.org/content/92/10/551.full; Laila Nurmohamed et al., "Outcome Following High-Dose Methotrexate in Pregnancies Misdiagnosed as Ectopic," *American Journal of Obstetrics and Gynecology* 205, no. 6 (2011), accessed December 20, 2011, http://www.ajog.org/article/S0002-9378(11)00903-3/fulltext.

24. Tom Blackwell, "Blackwell on Post: Study Links Autism, Diabetes in Pregnancy," National Post, October 27, 2011, http://news.nationalpost.com/2011/10/27/blackwell-on-health-study-links-autism-diabetes-in-pregnancy/.

25. Lars Heisterberg, MD, et al., "Sequelae of Induced First-Trimester Abortion," American Journal of Obstetrics and Gynecology (July 1986): 79.

26. C. V. Anath et al., "The Association of Placenta Previa with History of Cesarean Delivery and Abortion: A Meta-Analysis," American Journal of Obstetrics and Gynecology (November 1997): 1071–78.

27. "Induced Abortion and Subsequent Placenta Previa," American Association of Prolife Obstetricians and Gynecologists (AAPLOG), citing Thorp (OB GYN Survey 58, no. 1 [2002]), accessed January 4, 2012, http://www.aaplog.org/complications-of-induced-abortion/induced-abortion-and-placenta-previa/induced-abortion-and-subsequent-placenta-previa/.

28. Ibid.

29. Susan A. Cohen, "Repeat Abortion, Repeat Unintended Pregnancy, Repeated and Misguided Government Policies," Guttmacher Policy Review 10, no. 2 (Spring 2007), http://www.guttmacher.org/pubs/gpr/10/2/gpr100208.html.

30. F. Parazzini et al., "Reproductive Factors and the Risk of Invasive and Intraepithelial Cervical Neoplasia," British Journal of Cancer 59 (1989):805–9; H. L. Stewart et al., "Epidemiology of Cancers of the Uterine Cervix and Corpus, Breast and Ovary in Israel and New York City," Journal of the National Cancer Institute 37, no. 1:1–96; I. Fujimoto et al., "Epidemiologic Study of Carcinoma in Situ of the Cervix," Journal of Reproductive Medicine 30, no. 7 (July 1985): 535; C. LaVecchia et al., "Reproductive Factors and the Risk of Hepatocellular Carcinoma in Women," International Journal of Cancer 52 (1992): 351.

31. Joel Brind, "Comprehensive Review and Meta-Analysis of the Abortion/Breast Cancer Link," http://www.ncbi.nlm.nih.gov/pmc/articles/PMC1060338/?tool=pmcentrez.

32. L. A. Brinton et al., "Reproductive Factors in the Aetiology of Breast Cancer," British Journal of Cancer 47 (1983): 757–62. http://www.ncbi.nlm.nih.gov/pubmed/6860545

33. http://mediamatters.org/.

34. ""Daily Caller Promotes 'Grossly Inadequate' Study Linking Abortion and Breast Cancer," Media Matters for America, December 1, 2011, http://mediamatters.org/research/201112010016?frontpage, "Media Matters for America is a Web-based, "Who we are": "a not-for-profit, 501(c)(3) progressive research and information center dedicated to comprehensively monitoring, analyzing, and correcting conservative misinformation in the U.S. media."

35. M. Gissler et al., "Pregnancy-Associated Mortality after Birth, Spontaneous Abortion or Induced Abortion in Finland, 1987–2000," American Journal of Obstetrics and Gynecology 190 (2004): 422–27.

36. M. Gissler et al., "Pregnancy-Associated Deaths in Finland 1987–1994: Definition Problems and Benefits of Record Linkage," Acta Obsetricia et

Gynecolgica Scandinavica 76 (1997): 651–57; online summary, "Abortion Four Times Deadlier than Childbirth," *The Post-Abortion Review* 8, no. 2 (April–June 2000), Elliot Institute, http://afterabortion.org/2000/abortion-four-times-deadlier-than-childbirth/.

37. US Centers for Disease Control and Prevention, "Abortion Surveillance—United States, 2000," *Morbidity and Mortality Weekly Report* 52 (SS12), 32.

38. James A. Miller, "A Tale of Two Abortions," *Human Life International Reports,* March 1991, 1.

39. Brian Clowes, "Maternal Deaths Due to Abortion," *Facts of Life* (Human Life International, 2nd ed., June 2001).

40. Wanda Franz, "Abortion Associated with Heightened Mortality Rate, Study Reveals," National Right to Life (2002), www.nrlc.org/news/2002/NRL09/franz.html.

41. Elizabeth Ring-Cassidy and Ian Gentles, *Women's Health after Abortion: The Medical and Psychological Evidence,* 2nd ed. (Toronto: de Veber Institute, 2003), www.deveber.org.

42. Alfred Kinsey, cited in John Willke, *Abortion Questions and Answers* (Cincinnati, OH: Hayes Publishing, 1988), 169.

43. Mary Calderone, "Illegal Abortion as a Public Health Problem," *American Journal of Health* 50 (July 1960): 949.

44. Bernard Nathanson, *Aborting America* (New York: Doubleday, 1979), 193.

45. Rethinking Education About Life [REAL], UC San Diego, "Abortion Statistics," http://realweb.ifastnet.com/stats.html.

46. Bernard Nathanson, MD, *Aborting America,* 42.

47. Ibid. REAL, "Abortions Annually and Trends," Table 1, http://realweb.ifastnet.com/stats.html#deaths; also http://www.cdc.gov/nchs/releases/00facts/trends.htm

48. Germain Grisez, *Abortion: The Myths, the Realities, and the Arguments* (New York: Corpus Books, 1972), 70.

49. Carol Everett, personal conversation with the author and Frank Peretti, May 24, 1991.

50. Pamela Zekman, Pamela Warrick, "12 dead after abortions in state's walk-in clinics," Abortion Profiteers series, *Chicago Sun-Times, Nov 19, 1978,* http://dlib.nyu.edu/undercover/sites/dlib.nyu.edu.undercover/files/documents/uploads/editors/ChiSunTimes_1978Nov19_1.pdf.

51. Dennis Cavanaugh, "Effect of Liberalized Abortion on Maternal Mortality Rates," *American Journal of Obstetrics and Gynecology* (February 1978): 375.

52. David C. Reardon, *Aborted Women: Silent No More* (Westchester, IL: Crossway, 1987), 301.

53. "Key Facts about Abortion," Elliot Institute, n.d., www.afterabortion.org.

Chapter 12: Is Abortion Right When Pregnancy Presents Risks to the Mother's Life?

1. Landrum Shettles with David Rorvik, *Rites of Life* (Grand Rapids: Zondervan, 1983), 129.

2. "Pregnancy and Cancer" American Society of Clinical Oncology, May 2011, http://www.cancer.net/patient/coping/emotional+and+physical+matters/sexual+and+reproductive+health/pregnancy+and+cancer.

3. Ibid.

4. Hilary White, "No Case Where Abortion Was 'Necessary to Save Mom': Eminent Irish Oncologist," LifeSiteNews, February 22, 2012, http://www.lifesitenews.com/news/no-case-where-abortion-was-necessary-to-save-mom-eminent-irish-oncologist.

5. "There Is a High Chance of Two Happy Outcomes," *Irish Independent,* December 16, 2011, http://www.independent.ie/lifestyle/parenting/there-is-a-high-chance-of-two-happy-outcomes-2965911.html.

6. Lee-may Chen and Jonathan Berek, "Patient Information: Endometrial Cancer Diagnosis and Staging," Wolters Kluwer Health, accessed December 20, 2011, http://www.uptodate.com/contents/patient-information-endometrial-cancer-diagnosis-and-staging.

7. V. Seror et al., "Care Pathways for Ectopic Pregnancy: A Population-Based Cost-Effectiveness Analysis," *Fertility and Sterility* 87 (April 2007): 737–48.

8. Bill Fortenberry, "Ectopic Personhood," *The Personhood Initiative,* accessed December 20, 2011, http://www.personhoodinitiative.com/ectopic-personhood.html.

9. US Centers for Control and Prevention, *Morbidity and Mortality Weekly Report* 42 (SS-6), 73–85 (December 17, 1993; April 1984).

10. Bill Fortenberry, "Ectopic Personhood."

11. Laila Nurmohamed et al., "Outcome Following High-Dose Methotrexate in Pregnancies Misdiagnosed as Ectopic," *American Journal of Obstetrics and Gynecology* 205, no. 6 (2011): 533.e1–533.e3, http://www.ajog.org/article/S0002-9378(11)00903-3/fulltext.

12. B. Travert et al., "Population-Based Ectopic Pregnancy Trends, 1993–2007," *American Journal of Preventative Medicine* 40, no. 5 (May 2011): 556–60, abstract posted by US National Library of Medicine, National Institutes of Health, accessed December 9, 2011, http://www.ncbi.nlm.nih.gov/pubmed/21496755.

13. Ann Aschengrau Levin, "Ectopic Pregnancy and Prior Induced Abortion," *American Journal of Public Health* (March 1982): 253.

Chapter 13: Is Abortion Right When Pregnancy Is Due to Rape or Incest?

1. Jean Staker Garton, *Who Broke the Baby?* (Minneapolis, MN: Bethany House, 1979), 76.

2. Lawrence B. Finer, et. Al., Guttmacher Institute, "Reasons U.S. women Have Abortions; Quantitative and Qualitative Perspectives," Vol 37, No 3, Sepr 2005, http://www.guttmacher.org/pubs/journals/3711005.pdf.

3. Jane Orient, MD, "The Truth of Forcible Rape, or Public Hysteria," Association of American Physicians and Surgeons; http://www.wnd.com/2012/08/akin-not-far-off-base-in-rape-comment; also referenced, http://www.physiciansforlife.org/content/view/2255/26/.

4. John Willke, *Abortion Questions and Answers* (Cincinnati, OH: Hayes Publishing, 1988), 146–50.

5. Sue Reily, "Life Uneasy for Woman at Center of Abortion Ruling," *The Oregonian*, May 9, 1989.

6. Caroline Overington, "Jane Roe Wants to Make Legal History Again," *The Age,* June 21, 2003, www.theage.com.au/articles/2003/06/20/1055828492398.html.

7. *Feminists for Life Debate Handbook* (Kansas City, MO: Feminists for Life of America, n.d.), 14.

8. Frederica Mathewes-Green, "Ask the Victims," *Citizen Magazine 2000*, http://facelife.org/content/rapeincestcontent.htm.

Chapter 14: Do Birth Control Pills Cause Abortion?

1. Eugene F. Diamond, "Word Wars: Games People Play about the Beginning of Life," *Physician*, November–December 1992, 14–15. For more on this see also D. A. Grimes and R. J. Cook, "Mifepristone (RU-486)—An Abortifacient to Prevent Abortion?" *New England Journal of Medicine* 327 (1992): 1088–89; and D. A. Grimes, "Emergency Contraception—Expanding Opportunities for Primary Prevention," *New England Journal of Medicine*, 337 (1997): 1078–79.

2. Walter Larimore, MD, "Growing Debate about the Abortifacient Effect of the Birth Control Pill and the Principle of the Double Effect," *Ethics and Medicine* 16, no. 1 (January 2000), updated by the author October 1, 2004, and posted by Eternal Perspective Ministries, www.epm.org/pilldebate.html.

3. Peter Modica, "FDA Nod to 'Morning-After' Pill Is Lauded," *Medical Tribune News Service*, February 26, 1997.

4. Ibid.

5. *World*, March 8, 1997, 9.

6. Associated Press, "College Vending Machine Dispenses 'Plan B,'" *Washington Post,* February 7, 2012, http://www.washingtonpost.com/local/

college-vending-machine-dispenses-plan-b-120/2012/02/07/gIQAQhm-
TxQ_video.html.

Chapter 15: What about Disabled and Unwanted Children?

1. W. Peacock, "Active Voluntary Euthanasia," *Issues in Law and Medicine* (1987). Cited in John Willke, *Abortion Questions and Answers* (Cincinnati, OH: Hayes Publishing, 1988), 212.

2. S. E. Smith, "*Devaluing the Disabled Body,*" *This Ain't Livin'*, August 17, 2009, http://meloukhia.net/2009/08/devaluing_the_disabled_body.html.

3. Richard S. Olney, MD, MPH, et al., "Chorionic Villa Sampling and Amniocentesis: Recommendations for Prenatal Counseling," 1, US Centers for Disease Control and Prevention, *Morbidity and Mortality Weekly Report 44-(RR9),* July 21, 1995, http://www.cdc.gov/mmwr/preview/mmwrhtml/00038393. htm, accessed 12-29-2011.

4. Jack Canick, PhD, "A New Prenatal Blood Test for Down Syndrome (RNA)," Clinical Trial NCT00877292, December 20, 2011, US National Institutes for Health, Clinical Trials, accessed December 29, 2011, http://www.clinicaltrials.gov/ct2/show/NCT00877292?term=Down+Syndrome&rank=3.

5. "Diamond Blackfan Anemia, Genetics, and You," 2, US Centers for Disease Control and Prevention, accessed December 29, 2011http://www.cdc.gov/ncbddd/dba/documents/DBA_GENETICS.pdf.

6. Richard S. Olney, MD. MPH, et al., "Chorionic Villa Sampling and Amniocentesis: Recommendations for Prenatal Counseling," 1, http://www.cdc.gov/mmwr/preview/mmwrhtml/00038393.htm, accessed 12-29-2011.

7. David C. Reardon, *Aborted Women: Silent No More* (Westchester, IL.: Crossway, 1987), 172.

8. "Amniocentesis Complications"; 6-6-2012, http://www.nhs.uk/conditions/amniocentesis/pages/complications.aspx, accessed 9-12-2012.

9. Susan Kitching, *London Sunday Times,* February 11, 1990.

10. Kristina Chew, "Parents Awarded $3 Million after Daughter Born with Down Syndrome," Care to Make a Difference, March 12, 2012, http://www.care2.com/causes/parents-sue-after-daughter-born-with-down-syndrome.html.

11. Willke, *Abortion Questions,* 211.

12. It should be pointed out that 75 percent of babies with anencephaly are live births. See Monika Jaquier, "Report about the Birth and Life of Babies with Anencephaly," Anancephalie.info, March 7, 2006, http://www.anencephalie-info.org/e/report.php.

13. Matthew C. Hoffman, "Brazilian Anencephalic Baby Shatters Pro-Abortion Myths," June 5, 2008, *LifeSiteNews,* http://www.lifesitenews.com/news/archive/ldn/2008/jun/08060502; see also a blog by Myah, accessed January 4, 2012, http://babyfaithhope.blogspot.com/2009/03/39-days-old.html.

14. "Jesse Alexander Brand," Anencephalie, info, October 10, 2007, http://www.anencephalie-info.org/e/jesse.php.

15. "Coping with Grief," accessed December 30, 2011, ASFHelp.com/coping.

16. Alberto Guibilini and Francesca Minerva, "After-birth Abortion: Why Should the Baby Live?," *Journal of Medical Ethics* (March 2012), http://jme.bmj.com/content/early/2012/03/01/medethics-2011-100411.short. Also, Kristina Chew, "Parents Awarded $3 Million After Daughter Born With Down Syndrome," 3/12/12, http://www.care2.com/causes/parents-sue-after-daughter-born-with-down-syndrome.html

17. "Born Unwanted: Developmental Consequences for Children of Unwanted Pregnancies" (Planned Parenthood Federation of America, n.d.).

18. The Adoption Foundation, "Some Numbers in a Nutshell," accessed December 29, 2011, http://infant.adoption.com/newborn/some-numbers-in-the-nutshell.html.

19. Allison Tarmann, "International Adoption Rate in U.S. Doubled in the 1990s," *Population Reference Bureau*, January 2003, http://www.prb.org/Articles/2003/InternationalAdoptionRateinUSDoubledinthe1990s.aspx.

20. "Known Black Market Operations," accessed December 30, 2011, http://www.adopting.org/adoptions/black-market-adoption-search-sites-adoption-2.html.

21. Jessica Hopper, "Black Market Babies Seeking Answers through Facebook" (http://www.facebook.com/SeymourFenichelAdoptees), ABC News, February 15, 2011, http://abcnews.go.com/US/adoptees-illegal-baby-selling-ring-led-seymour-fenichel/story?id=12886993.

22. Christian Homes and Special Kids, http://chask.org/.

Chapter 16: Does Abortion Prevent Child Abuse?

1. *Report of the National Center of Child Abuse and Neglect,* US Department of Health and Human Services, 1973–1982.

2. US Department of Health and Human Services, "Child Maltreatment 2010," chap. 3, 30, Table 3-1, and chap. 4 , 58, accessed December 30, 2011, http://www.acf.hhs.gov/programs/cb/pubs/cm10/cm10.pdf#page=31.

3. Edward Lenoski, *Heartbeat* 3 (December 1980), cited in John Willke, *Abortion Questions and Answers* (Cincinnati, OH: Hayes Publishing, 1988), 140–41.

4. H. P. David et al., eds., *Born Unwanted: Developmental Effects of Denied Abortion* (Prague: Avicenum, Czechoslovak Medical Press, 1988); *American Psychological Association,* "Tribute to Henry P. David, 1923–2009," April 2010, http://www.apa.org/international/pi/2010/04/tribute-david.aspx.

5. "Abuse Risk Linked to Abortion," *Washington Times*, November 2, 2005, http://www.washingtontimes.com/news/2005/nov/02/20051102-110138-9468r/.

6. Priscilla K. Coleman, PhD, et al., "Induced Abortion and Child-Directed Aggression among Mothers of Maltreated Children," *The Internet Journal of Pediatrics and Neonatology*, Internet Scientific Publications, accessed December 30, 2011, http://www.ispub.com/journal/the-internet-journal-of-pediatrics-and-neonatology/volume-6-number-2/induced-abortion-and-child-directed-aggression-among-mothers-of-maltreated-children.html.

7. Philip G. Ney, "A Consideration of Abortion Survivors," *Child Psychiatry and Human Development* (Spring 1983): 172–73.

8. Philip G. Ney, "Relationship between Abortion and Child Abuse," *Canadian Journal of Psychiatry* (November 1979): 611–12.

9. Coleman, "Induced Abortion and Child-Directed Aggression."

10. Nancy Michels, *Helping Women Recover from Abortion* (Minneapolis, MN: Bethany House, 1988), 169–70.

11. Susan Hatters Friedman, MD, "Child Murder by Mothers: A Critical Analysis of the Current State of Knowledge and a Research Agenda," *American Journal of Psychiatry* 162, no. 9 (September 1, 2005), http://ajp.psychiatryonline.org/article.aspx?articleid=177747.

12. Peter Singer, *Rethinking Life and Death* (New York: St. Martin's Griffin, 1996), 217.

Chapter 18: What about Adoption?

1. Frederica Mathewes-Green, *Real Choices* (Sisters, OR: Multnomah, 1995), 19.

2. Stephen Ertelt, "British Survey Finds Overwhelming Majority of Women Regretted Abortions," September 12, 2006, LifeNews, http://www.lifenews.com/2006/09/12/nat-2579/.

3. Christina Dunigan, "Treating the Normal as if It's Abnormal, to Sell Abortions," *Real Choice blog*, July 30, 2011, http://realchoice.blogspot.com/2011/07/treating-normal-as-if-its-abnormal-to.html.

4. Testimonies of clinic workers in *The Abortion Providers*, a video produced by Pro-life Action League, Chicago. Confirmed by former abortion clinic owner Carol Everett, in private telephone conversation between her, Frank Peretti, and the author on May 24, 1991.

5. "Adoption Factbook Reveals New Domestic Adoption Study; Leads Discussion on Current State of Adoption" National Council for Adoption Press Release, May 24, 2011, https://www.adoptioncouncil.org/images/stories/Adoption_Factbook_Press_Release_Extended.pdf.

6. *1989 Adoption Factbook* (Washington, DC: The National Council for Adoption, June 1989), 158. These figures are relatively the same in 2000, per

phone conversation on May 8, 2000, with a representative of NCFA, confirming at least one million couples of childbearing age constitute the minimum adoption demand for newborns in the United States.

7. "Adoption Factbook Reveals New Domestic Adoption Study; Leads Discussion on Current State of Adoption," National Council for Adoption, May 24, 2011, https://www.adoptioncouncil.org/images/stories/Adoption_Factbook_Press_Release_Extended.pdf, accessed 12-30-2011.

8. Mathewes-Green, *Real Choices*, 14–15.

9. "How the Abortion Industry Sells Abortion by Exploiting Normal Feelings," August 5, 2011, Elliot Institute, *citing a Real Choice blogpost by Christian Dunigan*, http://afterabortion.org/2011/how-the-abortion-industry-sells-abortion-by-exploiting-normal-feelings/.

10. Cited in Charmaine Yoest, "Why Is Adoption So Difficult?" *Focus on the Family Citizen*, December 17, 1990, 10.

11. Paul Swope, "Abortion: A Failure to Communicate," *First Things*, April 1998, www.firstthings.com/ftissues/ft9804/articles/swope.html.

12. See www.bethany.org; www.cwa.org; www.preciouskids.org; www.adopting.com/info.html.

13. See http://encyclopedia.adoption.com/.

14. See "Relative Adoption," Advocates for Children and Families, http://www.adoptionflorida.org/relative.html.

15. Paul Swope, "Abortion: A Failure to Communicate," First Things, April, 1998, http://www.firstthings.com/article/2008/11/004-abortion-a-failure-to-communicate-49.

Chapter 19: Will God Forgive Abortions?

1. *Family Planning Perspectives*, July–August 1996, 12.

2. See http://www.healinghearts.org/index.php; http://afterabortion.org/help-healing/; call 1-888-486-HOPE for free confidential advice; resource list for post-abortion needs: www.afterabortion.org/resourc.html.

Chapter 21: How Can I Help Unborn Babies and Their Mothers?

1. Care Net's option line is 1-800-395-HELP (4357); online help at www.optionline.org.

2. See http://liveaction.org/get-involved; also, http://www.prolifeunity.com/index.php/C134/.

3. Eternal Perspective Ministries; www.epm.org; info@epm.org, 503-668-5200; 39085 Pioneer Blvd., Suite 206, Sandy, OR 97055.

4. For information on the National Memorial for the Unborn, see Leslie T. Dean, RN, "The Gift of Closure," *At the Center* (Autumn 2000), www.atcmag.com/v1n4/article6.asp; Kathy Norquist, "Memorial Rose Garden,"

Eternal Perspective Ministries, February 23, 2010, www.epm.org/articles/rosegard.html.

5. My book *ProLife Answers to ProChoice Arguments* is a thorough response to pro-choice claims, backed up with eight hundred citations.

6. Justice for All, http://www.jfaweb.org/Join_Us.html.

7. See Alcorn, *Pro-life Answers*, Appendix K: Pro-life Resources, 381–404; see http://www.epm.org/resources/2010/Apr/14/prolife-resource-list/. Also see note 2.

8. Randy Alcorn, "Does the Birth Control Pill Cause Abortions?," Eternal Perspective Ministries, March 15, 2010, www.epm.org/bcp.

9. See www.facebook.com/randyalcorn and www.twitter.com/randyalcorn.

10. Alexander Tsiaras, "Conception to Birth—Visualized!," December 2010, accessed January 2, 2012, http://www.ted.com/talks/alexander_tsiaras_conception_to_birth_visualized.html.

11. *The Advocate*, a publication of Live Action, http://www.liveaction.org/Advocate/.

12. Many pro-life resources are available online, including our organization's (Eternal Perspective Ministries) at http://www.epm.org/resources/2010/Apr/14/prolife-resource-list. All articles I've written and everything at our website are freely available for church and ministry use, including a small-group Bible study lesson at http://www.epm.org/resources/2009/Dec/22/choosing-and-defending-life/, and a complete sample of a creative pro-life church service and message at http://www.epm.org/resources/2010/Mar/21/rose-ceremony-remember-unborn/.

13. *180*, www.180movie.com; Alexander Tsiaras, "Conception to Birth—Visualized!" http://www.ted.com/talks/alexander_tsiaras_conception_to_birth_visualized.html; also DVD products at Heritage House, http://www.hh76.info/pro_life_products.asp?group_id=26.

14. *This Is Abortion*, http://www.abort73.com/videos/this_is_abortion/; or review www.abortionno.org/pdf/order.pdf. for other resources.

Appendix 1: Abortion in the Bible and Church History

1. Virginia Ramey Mollenkott, "Reproductive Choice: Basic to Justice for Women," *Christian Scholar's Review* (March 1988): 291.

2. James Hoffmeier, *Abortion: A Christian Understanding and Response* (Grand Rapids: Baker Book House, 1987), 46, 50; Eugene Quay, "Abortion: Medical and Legal Foundations," *Georgetown Law Review* (1967): 395, 420; Meredith G. Kline, "*Lex Talionis* and the Human Fetus," *Journal of the Evangelical Theological Society* (September 1977): 200–201.

3. Lawrence O. Richards, *Expository Dictionary of Bible Words* (Grand Rapids: Zondervan, 1985), 156–57.

4. Hoffmeier, *Abortion,* 62.

5. John Jefferson Davis, *Abortion and the Christian* (Phillipsburg, NJ: Presbyterian & Reformed, 1984), 52.

6. Kline, "*Lex Talionis,*" 193.

7. *A Pro-choice Bible Study* (Seattle, WA: Episcopalians for Religious Freedom, 1989).

8. Hoffmeier, *Abortion,* 53.

9. See George Grant, *Grand Illusions: The Legacy of Planned Parenthood* (Brentwood, TN: Wolgemuth & Hyatt, 1988), 190–91.

10. Quoted in Michael Gorman, *Abortion and the Early Church* (Downers Grove, IL: InterVarsity, 1982), 9.

11. John Calvin, *Commentary on Pentateuch,* cited in *Crisis Pregnancy Center Volunteer Training Manual* (Washington, DC: Christian Action Council, 1984), 7.

12. Dietrich Bonhoeffer, *Ethics* (New York: Macmillan, 1955), 131.

13. Karl Barth, *Church Dogmatics,* ed. Geoffrey Bromiley (Edinburgh: T. & T. Clark, 1961), 3:415, 3:418.

14. An excellent refutation of the various "Christian" pro-choice arguments is made by philosophy professor Francis Beckwith in "A Critical Appraisal of Theological Arguments for Abortion Rights," *Bibliotheca Sacra* (July–September 1991): 337–55.